MOONGLOW
Á GO-GO

Other Books by Joan Jobe Smith

Tales of an Ancient Go-Go Girl, Memoir: marJo Books, 2014 (USA)
Where the Stars at Night Are Big & Bright, Chapbook, Silver Birch Press,
   2014 (USA)
Charles Bukowski: Epic Glottis: His Art & His Women (& me), Literary
   Profile, Silver Birch Press, 2013 (USA)
Sequin Soul, Chapbook, Chance Press, 2010 (USA)
Joan's Own Good-4-YOU Cook Book, Pearl Editions, 2007 (USA)
Teatime @ the Bouquet Morale (w/Fred Voss), Chapbook Winner
   Nerve Cowboy 2006 Competition (USA)
Sparking, ragged EDGE Magsheets, 2005 (UK)
Picking the Lock on the Door to Paradise, Chapbook Winner Nerve
   Cowboy 1999 Competition (USA)
Bukowski Boulevard, Pearl Editions, 1999 (USA)
The Pow Wow Café, The Poetry Business/Smith/Doorstop Books, 1998 (UK
Born Not to Laugh at Tornadoes, Liquid Paper Press, 1997 (USA)
Love Birds (w/Fred Voss), Chiron Poetry 1st Prize Chapbook, 1997 (USA)
Heart Thread, Tears in the Fence Chapbook Winner, 1997 (UK)
a spy in a broccoli forest, Sheila-Na-Gig 1st Prize Chapbook, 1997 (USA)
Joan Teaches Fred to Cook Book, Pearl Limited Editions, 1996 (USA)
Modern Classic, Wormwood Review, 1996 (USA)
When the Movies Were Real, Sestet, Staple First Editions, 1995 (UK)
Trying on Their Souls for Size, Smith/Doorstop Books, 1994 (UK)
More Secrets About Beans, Feature Section Wormwood Review: 133, 1994 (USA
The Coolest Car in School, Pearl Editions, 1993 (USA)
The Honeymoon of King Kong & Emily Dickinson (w/Fred Voss), Zerx Press,
   1993 (USA)
Jehovah Jukebox, Event Horizon, 1993 (USA)
Two Poems: Ars Longa, Vita Brevis, Carniverous Arpeggio Press, 1992 (UK)
Fred & Joan, Guillotine Press, 1990 (USA)
Why Robert Wagner Married Natalie Wood, Feature: Wormwood Review: 177,
   1990 (USA)
The Habit of Wishing (w/Ann Menebroker & Rosemary Cappello), Goldermood
   Press, 1976 (USA)

Moonglow á Go-Go

New and Selected Poems

Joan Jobe Smith

The New York Quarterly Foundation, Inc.
New York, New York

NYQ Books™ is an imprint of The New York Quarterly Foundation, Inc.

The New York Quarterly Foundation, Inc.
P. O. Box 2015
Old Chelsea Station
New York, NY 10113

www.nyq.org

First Edition

Set in New Baskerville

Layout and Design by Raymond P. Hammond

Cover Art: "Spray-gun Proto-Psychedelia, 1963" by Avner Ray Jobe

Library of Congress Control Number: 2017915774

ISBN: 978-1-63045-039-7

Dedicated to Marilyn Johnson
Exquisite, Prodigious Godmother of Pearl, Incomparable,
Eloquent Artiste
Friend, Mother, Wife Extraordinaire—
with unbounding
and eternal
Affection and Respect.

Acknowledgments

The author thanks with much gratitude the editors of the following publications in which many of her poems appeared:

A Common Thread, The Aldeburgh Poetry Festival Anthology (UK), *Ambit* (UK), *A New Geography of Poets, Another City, The Bastille* (Paris, France), *The Best of California Women Writers, Bete Noire* (UK), *Beyond the City of Angels, Blades, Bloc Notes 59* (Italy), *Blood to Remember—American Poets on the Holocaust, Bukowski Anthology, Bukowski Boulevard, Bukowski-on-Wry, Charles Bukowski; Shakespeare N'a Jamais Fait Ca* (Paris, France), *Chiron Review, Circe's Lament, Columbia Review, Counterfeit Crank* (UK), *Cultural Weekly, Epic Glottis: Charles Bukowski: His Art, His Women (& me), Eureka* (Sweden), *The Forward Book of Poetry* (UK), *Georgia Review, The Giant Book of Poetry, Grand Passion—Poets of L.A. & Beyond, How Dirty Girls Get Clean, Inkshed* (UK), *Jehovah Jukebox, Judas Hole* (UK), *Like a Girl: Perspectives on Feminine Identity, Literature & Its Writers, Los Angeles Times, Prism: An Interdisciplinary Journal for Holocaust Educators, Medula Livros* (Portugal), *The Morning Star* (UK), *Nerve Cowboy, New York Quarterly, The North* (UK), *The Outlaw Bible of American Poetry, Pearl, Picking the Lock on the Door to Paradise, The Pow Wow Café* (UK), *Philadelphia Poets, Prop* (UK), *Purr, Quincunx* (UK), *Rattle, The Reater* (UK), *The Rialto* (UK), *Risk Behaviour* (UK), *San Diego Union, San Pedro River Review, Sestet* (UK), *The Shop* (Ireland), *Silver Anthology, Smith Knoll* (UK), *SpotLit, Surfer Magazine, Swallow Dance, Tales of an Ancient Go-Go Girl, Tears in the Fence* (UK), *Turpin's Cave* (UK), *The Wormwood Review*

"Because I Was Born Laughing" first appeared in Silver Birch Press "Me, As a Child" Series, April, 2015.

"11 a.m. Just like Edward Hopper's Redhead" first appeared in Silver Birch Press "Where I Live" Series, March, 2015.

"Why Isn't There a 10th Muse Named Margie?" first appeared in Silver Birch Press "Mythic" Series, November, 2014.

Foreword

I like to joke with Joan that she could have been Kim Novak's body double on the set of *Pal Joey*. (It's just possible. Bear in mind that Joan is a big Sinatra fan.) And I like to imagine a movie after-life for nightclub dancer "Linda English," in which things didn't work out with Joey, she found happiness only with her fourth marriage, in the meantime taking jobs as a go-go girl at tough Los Angeles area clubs and beer bars during the years of social upheaval 1965-72; and, under the name Joan Jobe Smith, writing these wonderfully engaging poems. Linda's story is Joan's in essence—the *ingenue* who toughens up in the face of whatever mankind throws at her, becoming a woman of the world, able to reflect upon her multiple roles within the times she's lived through with hard-won compassion and poignancy. And with pop-culture allusive art. For Joan's poems habitually reference movies and movie stars in ironic parallel to workaday realities, or celebrate their sustaining fantasies: "we imagined we wore marabou,/ danced the Continental with/ Fred Astaire as he crooned/ 'Cheek to Cheek' so we didn't care/ when a drunk reached to cop a feel" ("And the Ladies of the Fred Astaire Fan Club").

Of course, her writing has an inherent soundtrack, teeming as it is with snippets from the Great American Songbook, pop songs of the 1950s dawn of Rock n'Roll ("Darling, You Send Me") forwards to its 1960s "L.A. Woman" heyday and on into the "I-Will-Survive" of 1970s disco. But it's not escapist, and rarely hedonistic; rather, there's an underlying social dimension. Almost all of the poems in *Jehovah Jukebox* can be read that way, as can other Go-Go poems such as "Feminist Arm Candy for the Mafia and Frank Sinatra." Sindy's demands for union recognition to protect the "dancing workhorses" are ignored, so she escapes the Playgirl Club for Las Vegas, only to return six months later, "eyes swollen from a day-ago beating,/ nostrils cracked from snorting cocaine, eyeballs red from day/ time pot smoking and a slipped disc because they'd made her/ wear 50-pound headpieces". Its conclusion, "in turn-on, tune-out 1969, God only knew," the last three words conjuring up The Beach Boys' song, brilliantly juxtaposes this vignette of physical abuse/ economic exploitation with the surrounding (only seemingly liberationist) pop culture.

All of Joan's writings, whether poems or prose, books and chapbooks, form a continuum of plain-speaking style and woman-centered experience, what is essentially a very large discontinuous fictional-autobiographical sequence. So her subjects range over diverse eras, recounting the vagaries of family life, marriages, abusive relationships, raising children and caring for (in Joan's case) a beloved terminally-ill mother. Alongside, her literary career was first fledged as an MFA graduate of the University of California at Irvine, then as a founding editor of long-running *Pearl* magazine (from 1974, re-launched in the mid-1980s, so called after a Janis Joplin album). A crucial early mentor was Marvin Malone of *Wormwood Review,* whose influential little magazine gave her several special sections over the years (and in whose pages she first "met" her future "good husband" Fred Voss).

But it's Charles Bukowski who looms largest, whom she once described as "my main objet d'art, cause celebre and entrée to becoming a writer." What did she learn from her correspondence and occasional meetings with him? For the full answer, see her memorializing *Bukowski Boulevard* (1999), *Epic Glottis* (2012), where you can sample the vegetarian chili Joan made for him in 1975, and the "Beer Can in the Garden" chapter of *Tales of an Ancient Go-Go Girl* (2015). But in brief, acknowledging that Bukowski's is a harder-bitten art, I'd say she learned not to sugar-coat the pill in swallowing existence whole, bitterness or humor being equally valid responses, that writing should be emotionally honest not stylistically pretentious.

Where Joan herself is concerned, I'm grateful to her (and Fred Voss) for over twenty years thus far of friendship, hospitality, and transatlantic exchanges. She deserves a Lifetime Achievement Award. Her poems seem as inescapably Californian as the Beach Boys, the Doors, or her sometime friend Bukowski. But they point out the grindingly hard life realities behind Californian Dreaming. However, they're also are affirmative, suggesting (like the movies and great music) how important fantasy is in blissfully augmenting harsh existence. And so I like to imagine Joan driving her beloved Volkswagens down palm tree-fringed *Bukowski Boulevard* in an Endless

Summer, her *Sequin Soul* switching fictional freeways as smoothly as her poems do the decades, all her many stories rushing past. To first time readers of JJS, I'd say delicious confections lie within. I can't wait to sample these poems again, this artful selection from the "strange and hectic life" of the Long Beach Lady Go-Go. Enjoy.

—Jules Smith, 2017
Times Literary Supplement Critic and Author of *Art, Survival and So Forth: The Poetry of Charles Bukowski* (Wrecking Ball Press, 2000)

Contents

Moonglow á Go-Go

"We all shine on...like
the moon and stars and the sun...
we all shine on...come on and on and on..."

—John Lennon

Moonglow á Go-Go

Come on baby, it's June!
Dance us to the moon!
Light our fire, smite our dire while I swoon
seeing you in your blue suede shoes, white
sport coat and a pink carnation, me in my tight
tight red dress, high heel sneakers so we can go-
go shake rattle and roll, rock around the clock as
you drive your cherry-cherry pie Buick 69 fast
past Route 66, the yellow rose of Texas, gals in
Kalamazoo, Mississippi mud, New York, New York,
beyond the sea, smoke upon the water, blue heaven
and the twelfth of never somewhere over the rainbows.

Only you can love me tender, dance me where stardust
trombones moan us weightless as we sway sambas
cha-cha high and low-down in outer space with Mars
Saturn and Jupiter in our face, the stars a tiara prize
in my hair, moonglow á go-go in your devil moon eyes
as we foxtrot a boogie-woogie wa-wa-wa-Watusi sighs
and do-wop and be-bop-a-lula like a sister Lucy.

Call me li'l' Darlin', kiss me once, kiss me twice my
60-minute man as saxes slap our backsides.

Waltz me in the Milky Way, far-out and out of sight
tango, dip me a total eclipse as our backbones slip
and you light my fire, smite my dire, kiss again my lips
begin the beguine dancing me, prancing me, enchanting me
crooning and spooning me April and May and June
with wings of angels on our shoes

all the way to

the moon.

Because I Was Born Laughing

My mother had this picture taken of just us two in a
photo booth in Paris, Texas, February, 1940, to give to
her rich cousin Mae who was related to Jesse James to
show me some day what my mother looked like who
couldn't take care of me, she had to go to work, be a
waitress, so she gave me away to her rich cousin Mae
related to Jesse James because Mae had a big ranch and
plenty of money for a nanny to take care of me because
I was born laughing, I was not born dead like the doctors
said, because I was born feet first and stopped being born
at the knees for 14 hours till my feet and legs turned purple.
And because I was born laughing instead of being dead,
the doctors said I'd never be right in the head because of
lack of oxygen to my brain those 14 hours and I'd never
walk or talk or feed myself, button buttons, tie my shoes,
get a job and earn my keep, be a wife or mother because
I was born laughing and that proved their theory that I was
not all there—my laughter merely neurological spasms and
my laughter so depressed my father, he went away (but he'd
later come back) and, so, there I am in that photo, only
four weeks old as my bereaving mother hugs me tightly
in her arms in the photo booth, the first photo ever taken
of just us two to give to her Jesse James cousin Mae to
show me some day (if I can understand) because I was
born laughing, laughing in that photo because I'm happy,
surely knowing that my mother is beautiful, so very happy
because I can feel her heartbeat, hear her sighs telling me
she'll come back to get me in just 3 weeks because her heart
will nearly break (she'll tell me when I'm grown) because
she'll miss me which is what my mother did. All because
I was born laughing.

Why, Oh, Why Do I Write Poetry?

My mother said I was "tetched" in her Texas lingo
when I began at age 8 to write poetry, Alice in my own
wonderland and then I won a Red Cross safety poster
contest with my rhyming aphorism "Always wait for
the green/And you will become a Safety Queen" and
when they put it on a billboard in our town, my father
agreed with my mother that I was tetched to waste my
time jotting rhyme because the prize I won, a faux gold
watch wouldn't fit my wrist till I was 20. So I stopped
rhyming until I was 15 and fell in love with Elizabeth
Barrett Browning and wrote a poem to a boy who fell
in love with me but I didn't love him: "Amalgamated
bricks/that's what you are/an uninhabitable planet/so
far, far, far" but he did not heed my mixed metaphor
and made me date him anyway so I wrote poetry no
more until I was a mother at age 18: "at 16 I dreamed
of you, dear baby/and now you are here/lying so near/
to my heart/as I kiss the tip of you/your newborn head/
warm crayon upon me/as I wonder what color/you will be"
but on and on Life went on: 2 divorces, 2 more babies,
go-go nite clubs made me too tired, wired to write poetry
until I was 32 and feeling blue married to a hippie and
pondered What's it all about? No Shakespeare sonnets
helped nor did Whitman, Bob Dylan, Dylan Thomas
nor Ted Hughes's baby ewes, Neruda's musings. But
Angelou's sagacity, audacity, and Sylvia's lamentations
inspired some solace; so did Charles Bukowski's drunken
exclamations as I wrote and wrote and re-wrote my poetry
self-conscious jottings until I was age 37 and stopped to
write my prose thesis for grad school and then at age 45
I wrote poetry again, bereaved when my mother died
and I never stopped writing poetry ever again while I
married a poet who never wonders the worried way I do
Why do I write poetry? Am I tetched? Have a screw loose?
Do I do the work of the devil or do internship for immortality?
Do Muses dance on my head? Erato whisper just for me?

What's the use of these self-conscious jottings, the reams
of words I've composed, piling up pages like a sky-high
paper Colossus of Rhodes? Am I a wastrel? A drama queen?
Oh, I know: poetry's something to do while I wait for the green.

Green

Everything was green when I was a teen,
our house was green, the fern wallpaper,
the orange and lemon trees, the grassy back
and front yards were green, my father's Ford
Fairlane was two-tone green, the gingham
kitchen curtains my mother sewed on her new Singer
were green, the spinach, collards, and green beans
we ate were green, even my high school colors and
the hassock was green I sat upon in my bedroom
to watch out my window the cool guys drive by
in their lowered Mercs and Chevies, Bill Flynn's
St. Patrick's Day plaid shirt green, green everywhere
and I hated green and vowed when married everything
would be aquamarine and for years just about
everything was, the tv and drapes, the Naugahyde
sofa, even my unbreakable Melmac plates and
saucers had tiny aquamarine flowers on them
even though there were no aquamarine flowers
anyplace else in the world and now everything
in my house is green, the ivy painted on my
mother's old Franciscan dinnerware green,
the apples and avocados in the bowl are green
the goblets we drink from are green, the split pea
soup I simmer on the stove green, the broccoli
I steam green, the napkins and tablecloth, the
placemats, the lamps, the sheets and pillows,
the towels, the Christmas lights and the walls are
the color of the rain forests, the ceiling painted
pearl white to resemble thick cumulus clouds.

I guess I lied about hating green.

Green When It Rained

When it rained was when my mother sang
her sweetest as she cooked supper in the
kitchen. "Ohh," she'd whisper, fogging up
the window with her breath. "Look at the
beautiful rain, how green the world, the
leaves, when it rains. Rain now means
food to eat next year. Do you understand?"
No, I didn't. We lived in southern California
in the 1950s in the eternal plentitude midst of
supermarkets, farmers markets selling food
grown in nearby cornfields and orange groves.
Dairies with fat cows surrounded us, jingling
ice cream men and bakery trucks filled with
sweets and hot bread drove up and down
our streets. In between her songs, Amapola,
my pretty little poppy, you'll never know
how much I love you, always, she'd tell me
of yellow Texas droughts and brown famine
how she searched shadow gullies for greens
when she was a little girl, stole corn, peaches
and pecans from rich folks' fields and orchards.
I'd never gone hungry nor had to steal or search
for my food and her sweet soprano tales of
hunger filled me with so much wanting that come
suppertime as I mashed the buttery, Texas-style
potatoes, I scraped spotless the pot with the spoon
to lick every speck, grateful to all the gods
of cornucopia, ambrosia and green Mother Rain.

The Hollow Cost

My mother told me about the hollow cost
one Saturday morning as I lay
in her bed beside her where I read
comic books while she moaned
for just forty more winks, it her
day off from the Payless Café
and when she finally yawned
stretched and woke, after I'd
turned the Little Lulu pages
as loudly as I could, sometimes
she told me stories about when
she was a little girl in Texas
riding horses, milking cows,
cooking on a wood-burning stove.
But that one morning she cleared her throat
the way she always did before she scolded me
and she told me she had something to tell me
that I should hear from my mother
hunger
gas showers
shaven-headed women
sixty-pound men
human-skin lampshades
the war so much more
than white oleo
FDR speeches on the radio
letters from my Army medic father in Algeria. Oh,
how you wish you had never heard
some of the things your mother told you
that six million were more
than all the stars in the sky
on a clear, winter night.

Endless River of Silvery Moons

Everything was silver when I was a kid with
Hi Ho Silver! and Lone Ranger silver bullets
as silver airplanes flew off to World War 2,
all of our money silver dimes and dollars,
movie stars on the big silver screen smiling
silver teeth wore silver streaked hair, drove cars
made of silver-hump bumpers, big-grinning grills
and hubcaps silver glitter swirls beneath silvery fog
sunsets in San Francisco while I set the supper table
with silver forks, spoons and knives and sometimes
after they tucked me into bed my mother and father
in the living room cheek to cheek danced in the dark
while Artie Shaw's 78rpm clarinet played "Stardust"
and I watched, waited to grow up to live my life, too,
beside the light of an endless river of silvery moons.

Good Wives Don't Drive

My father refused to teach my mother
to drive his car, he said it wasn't ladylike
in 1949, a woman driver was no better
than a streetwalker; she was to take the bus
and be a good wife like his mother was

so my mother took secret driving lessons
the instructor man coming every day
in a grey sedan to show her how to
let out the clutch just right so the car
wouldn't jerk, how to work the choke
and the radio, headlights, make
turn signals, arm bent up for right
straight out for left, down for slow
me in the backseat watching as we drove

the L.A. streets: Firestone, Rosemead,
Sunset Boulevard, Pico, Wilshire, La Brea,
Lakewood, Atlantic and Santa Fe and the day
she got her driver's license she bought herself
a green 1939 Ford coupé and waited in the
front seat in the driveway for my father to come
home then honked the horn when he arrived

and said, *Hey, Handsome, need a ride?*

Listening to the Radio

My father had a hairy chest, just like
the Hairy Ape in Eugene O'Neil's play
I'd seen in the movies and I wondered
if someday I'd have a hairy chest, too,
since I looked so much like him:
thin lips, high forehead, pale skin.

"Of course not," he said.
"You're a girl. And I'm a man."

And I wondered if I really was a girl
going to be a woman someday like
they all said, looked down at my
chest, flat like his, accordion
boned like his.

"What would happen," I asked him,
"if I did grow hair on my chest?"

"Shhh," he whispered, biting his
fingernails the way I did, too,
"I'm listening to the radio."

Steve Bilko Taught Me How to Spit

In sixth grade when my little girlfriends all began
en masse to unfurl plump blossoming pink into
woman cake and I stayed 4-foot-2, weighed 48
pounds and liked to play baseball instead of kiss
boys, the girls teased me that I was a midget or
maybe even a hermaphrodite so playing short stop
was the right place for me shortstopped like I was
in time as I ran in and out of inner and outer field
catching pop flies, shortstopping line drives and
swinging around to tag the runner stealing third base.
Then at home on weekends while my workaholic
father fixed stuff in his garage, I'd sneak to watch the
Pacific Coast League on tv: the Los Angeles Angels,
the Hollywood Stars, learned how to kick my feet
into the dust at home plate, wipe some dust on my
bat and swing wide and swift like Steve Bilko who
was Southern California's answer to Babe Ruth and
I taught myself to spit like Steve Bilko, make it flip
in the air before it hit the dirt and when my team won
I put my fingers in my mouth and whistled so loud it
made church bells ring in the next town. It was good
to keep my mind off all that troubling hermaphrodite
stuff with all my short stopping during that short
stopping of time when the moon and stars didn't yet
know my name or where to find me to turn me into a
woman and later it all paid off when I was a cocktail
waitress all grown up in a swanky hotel and met Joe
DiMaggio and asked while I served him a cappuccino
Whatever happened to Steve Bilko? and Joe DiMaggio
asked me while eyeing my cleavage and fishnet stockings:
YOU know who Steve Bilko is? Yes, I growled like a
tough sixth grade boy who plays shortstop: Steve Bilko
taught me how to spit that day when the score was 1–0
in the bottom of the 9th and Steve Bilko hit a grand slam.
I don't know for sure if Steve Bilko ever did that but it
made Joe DiMaggio laugh and give me his autograph.

Why Robert Wagner Married Natalie Wood

Robert Wagner lived in my closet
the summer I was 14. Between movies,
bored with Bel Aire and the Riviera, he
lived amongst my skirts and sweaters
and pedal pushers and sat with me
next to my shoes on the floor and
talked to me about being grown up
where the summer before I'd talked to
my dolls about castles and ever afters.

One day my father found Robert Wagner
in my closet, his photograph actually
from *Photoplay* tacked to the closet
door and my father saw the lipstick
kiss (Cutex's "Roses in the Snow")
next to Robert Wagner's smile. My
father didn't know what to think of me,
he said, and neither did I, feeling
strange and dreary as I would
years later from postpartum blues
so I removed Robert Wagner from the
closet and glued him in a scrapbook and
didn't look at him again for 40 years.

That's why he married Natalie Wood.

Heartthrobs

My Aunt Louis subscribed to *Photoplay*
wrote fan letters and kept a movie star
scrapbook for so long that she began to
hallucinate. Boldface lie, my father said,
but I believed my Aunt Louise's story that
the movie star Richard Egan had fallen
head-over-heels in love with her, drove
all the way from Hollywood to Colton,
California, to meet her Saturday afternoons
at the chili dog stand on Mt. Vernon Boulevard.
Just to hold her hand, nothing else,
my Aunt Louise, only 16, swore to her daddy,
a hot-headed Texas railroad man, who got out
his pistol and cleaned it and loaded it and
tried to sneak up on Richard Egan at the
chili dog stand to catch him in the act
with his little girl. But my grandpa always
got there too late, Richard Egan just
having driven away just moments before
back to L.A. in his red '54 Coupe de Ville.
Someday, someday, my grandpa would say,
I'm gonna get me that slippery son of a bitch
and my father would say, Jesus Christ, if this
don't beat all and go outside to grind his teeth.
Later, on our way back home to Long Beach
my father'd say if Louise were his daughter,
teenager or not, he'd get out his belt and
wallop some sense into her butt and I
knew that he would so I never told him when
Robert Wagner began peeking into my
bedroom window on nights the moon was full.

Cheatin' Hearts

Your cheatin' hearts will tell on you
Marion, Naomi and I
sang-shouted into the night
out my front door in 1955
during a pouring-down rainstorm
so's to be heard by Tommy, Bobby and Millard
across the street inside Tommy's house
with the lights out, our folks gone

and then Tommy, Bobby and Millard
sang-shouted louder to be heard
over the roars of thunder
Your cheatin' hearts will make you weep
while the glow-dots of their cigarettes
let us know they lay smoking on the floor
as they looked out Tommy's front door at us
as we struck matches in the dark
pretending to be smoking, too,
shivering in our pajamas.

That summer Naomi would fall in love
with Tommy, Marion with Millard,
Bobby would give me my first kiss
in the back seat of a '55 Chevy
at a drive-in movie, then in August Naomi
would take Millard away from Marion
marry him in 11th grade in September
and Marion, Tommy, Bobby and I
would marry others
Millard would leave Naomi and their 2 kids
for another woman, Tommy go to prison for drugs
and die young of lung cancer, Bobby, Millard
and Naomi disappear
and Marion and I become comadres

and finally when the rain began to pour down harder
we, the Patsy Clines
and they, the Hank Williamses
had to close the front doors
so's to keep ourselves
and the carpets dry.

SH-BOOM! Life Is but a Dre-eam

In high school Millard took Midol
to get high on and I thought
he was either crazy or a
hermaphrodite.

In 11th grade he married
my girlfriend Naomi who always wore
Sarah Coventry chokers to hide
the hickies on her neck Millard gave her
and was always telling me how I'd have
more boyfriends if I wore mascara.

The day they dropped out of high school
because they got married
Millard threw his stinky gym shoes
into the trash can on Senior Square
and in the book locker Naomi and I shared
left next to a dried-up baloney sandwich
was this note:

  "Dear MISS Jobe; on our first night
    Millards' folks put cracker
    crumbs in our bed. Ha. Ha.
    Millard teases me
    How wer'e gonna spend at least
    5$ a week for
    Vasaleen and you know whats!
    When you see Miss Roach tell her for me
    her study hall stinks and so does she!
    It sure is fun being marryed.
    SH-BOOM!
    Sinserly;
      MRS. Millard G. Glodson, Sept 29, 1955"

How Women Dance When They Dance with Each Other

Teaching me to jitterbug when I was the size
of a sack of potatoes, my mother slid me
through her legs spread wide apart, tossed me
in the air and caught me until she had to stop,
sit down and catch her breath

and then at 13 my girlfriend Marion Caudillo
taught me Mexican dances, the flamenco,
the hat dance in her living room, our
hands on our hips as we stomped our
heels on the wooden floor until
the dishes in the cupboards rattled
two Carmens pretending we wore black
lacy mantillas and flaming magenta skirts
instead of Levi's and T-shirts
neither of us wanting to be the boy

then Kay and me decades later
disco dancing in the rain
beside her van in the parking lot
the radio roaring the Bee Gees
"Stayin' Alive" each of us trying to lead,
getting wet, our curly hair frizzing,
our feet cold, our dancing becoming
arm wrestling tug of war trying to lead, win
and prove who was the best friend and wisest
dancer laughing drunk on white wine
shouting "Let ME lead!" in all that wet, happy rain.

The Gonad Story

At 15, anxious for my first diamond engagement
ring, I said Yes, I'd marry Jackie Lewis who'd just
quit high school to join the Coast Guard. I figured
when Jackie came home for Christmas with the
diamond ring, I'd wear it a few days to show off
to my girlfriends and then tell Jackie a Good Story
why I couldn't marry him. But the night before he
left for boot camp, I fixed him dinner (my parents
working late) and right after eating, Jackie lay down
on his stomach on my father's sofa in the den, placed
his hands between his legs and moaned: "Ohh—my
gonads. Ohh—my blue balls. Help me, help me,"
he moaned, reaching for my hand to help massage
the pain away that throbbed between his legs.
But I was only 15, had only been kissed two times
and didn't know about gonads even when he called
them testicles and begged me: "Help me, help me…"
So I ran to the telephone to call an ambulance. "No,
no," Jackie moaned. "Only YOU can help me—" So
I ran to the bathroom for aspirin, to the kitchen for
a glass of water to splash in poor Jackie's face. So
Jackie got up and limped home and come Christmas,
he neither phoned nor gave me a diamond engagement
ring. He went back to his old girlfriend Gloria who had
big boobs and I'd become engaged four more times, be
married twice, a go-go girl for five years when I finally
figured out the plot of Jackie Lewis's convoluted, con-
trived Gonad Story—a story as old as the trilobites who
first whispered it, same story later painted in Cro-Magnon
caves—that lecherous little male chauvinist pig plagiarist.

General Eisenhower

I hated how my father teased me about
my arched, Maybelline-darkened
Audrey Hepburn flare-arched eyebrows
he smeared some mornings at breakfast
to show me my eyebrows didn't look
as real as I thought

and I hated how he tucked
my Kim Novak spit curls behind my ears
straightening the curls, making me
look like the little girl at 15
he still thought me to be

and how he called my black, tight
Elizabeth Taylor capri pants cheap
and Elvis a hick
Little Richard and Fats Domino ridiculous
while all the while
he was so out of style
with his '40s Glenn Miller
wire-rimmed glasses
instead of Ivy Leaguer tortoise shell

and his clip-on bowtie
because a Windsor knot choked
his big Adam's apple
and his old World War 2
Eisenhower jacket and khakis
when all the cool guys wore
James Dean white T-shirts and Levi's

and while the cool guys picked me up for dates
in their lowered Mercs and Chevies
Bill Haley and the Comets roaring on the radio
my father chain-smoked Luckies
while his Artie Shaw 78s played

and he cursed those cool guys
and my generation in general
to a future of prison, famine, pestilence
and down-on-our-knees penitence
for our lack of decency
and common sense.

Kar Klub Kween

I still wonder why the car club guys picked me
for their Queen. I'd like to think it was because
they thought me cute but my girlfriend who knew
someone who knew some of the car club guys told me
they only picked me because my father
an auto-body man with his own shop might give them
discounts which he didn't because not only
was he a tightwad but he hated teenagers
thought all of us spoiled rotten
especially the guys, those no-good hot-rodders
who got to go to high school instead of having to
go off to the Civil Conservation Corps like my
father did in the Depression to support his mother.
So my father didn't like it one bit that the car club guys
picked me, he said the pictures of me in the
newspapers made me look like a dime-a-dance girl
said No, I couldn't go to Hollywood at midnight
Friday with the car club guys to go talk
on Huggy Boy's rock 'n' roll radio show.
I had an 11 o'clock curfew
and from then on it would be ten.

It was nerve-wracking listening to all that
when I had so much to worry about then, worry
if I could stop biting my fingernails in time
for the car club show in July, worry about being cute

and for the next 200 years of my life
that was to be a hectic and strange one
the wondering about whether or not
I did or did not possess the proper qualifications
and mysterious qualities to be justly picked
as someone's, anyone's Car Club Queen
became the very least
although the sweetest
of all my worries.

The Coolest Car in School

Wearing a white chiffon waltz-length gown with
seed pearls across the bodice and white gardenias
on my wrist I went to my junior prom with Nick
Turner in the leather aquamarine leather tuck 'n'
roll upholstered back seat of Tinker Christensen's
white '56 Olds, Tinker taking my girlfriend Jan in
the front seat, Tinker's Olds the coolest car in school,
Tinker waxing, polishing, customizing it every night
after his job at the supermarket, the four of us cruising
in it, actually cruising, listing like a yacht in tropical seas,
trade wind-blown as a schooner in moon rivers down
Firestone Boulevard in that lowered, white-glowing
car, all of us glowing, Jan in powder blue taffeta,
Tinker in a powder blue sports coat, Nick Turner in
a white one, on our way to the prom and then the
Moulin Rouge in Hollywood where even the movie
stars envied that car and then on our way home, gliding
in our barge along the Nile of the Hollywood Freeway,
the moon our wish-lamp, the stars our diamond dust,
Nick Turner, without asking, surprised me by kissing
my naked back, smack in-between my bare shoulder blades
and then later, when all grown up, I would ride in Mercedes
Benzes, T-Birds, Corvettes and limos, Mustangs and
Porsches, a red Pantera, a black XKE and a silver Lincoln
Continental and guys as handsome or more handsome than
Nick Turner would wine and dine me but never again
would it be like that and never again would the moon,
pearls or gardenias glow as silvery white or a '56 Olds shine
in the night as that night when our eyes were as young
and aquamarine as Tinker's leather tuck 'n' roll.

The
Coolest
Car
In School

Joan Jobe Smith

Burning Alive with Stars

You'd just turned 18, big for your age, wanted to
be a cop. A Good Cop. You drove a '52 royal blue
Chevy with sun visor because light hurt your baby
blue eyes (back then in 1957 sunglasses weren't cool,
grown-ups would've thought you a Beatnik). You
took me to drive-in movies, bought me hot fudge
sundaes, read to me *Peyton Place*—the dirty parts—
but I didn't get it, so I read to you *The Diary of Anne
Frank* and when I wept, you held my hand. You
said we were engaged to be engaged even though
you never told me you loved me, said we'd get
married next Valentine's Day or in June or maybe
after you joined the army, went to college, became
a cop. A Good Cop. You were so wise and worldly,
knew the latest technology, could fine tune treble
and bass knobs of my Magnavox hi-fi LPs, made
Sinatra's "In the Wee Small Hours of the Morning"
warm and mellow. Then one midnight, my parents
away, you said, "Let's take a shower together, stand
together wet and naked." But I didn't follow you, didn't
come to you when you called my name and when
you came out, your young strong muscles sparkling
wet wrapped in a towel and you asked me "Why
didn't you?" I covered my eyes with my hands. I
was only 17 and had never seen such a thing as you
and I was too ashamed to tell you that my skin was
only marshmallow and was burning alive with stars.

Good, Good Vibrations

Over my father's shoulders, a screeching eagle, soared
the sound of "Gee" from the car radio as he drove his car
December 1953 down the mountain of California snow.
"GEE!" the first rhythm and blues I'd ever heard. "Gee,
love that girl..." sang the Crows jerking me alive with
good vibrations while making my father jerk with rage,
say Jesus Christ! What the hell's THAT? profanity he saved
for damning traffic jams, Communists and H-bombs and
as he reached to twist the radio knob, I jiggled in the
back seat of his '53 Ford my first getting-grown-up dance
feeling the good vibrations, vibrations Salome flung veils to,
Jane Avril Moulin Rouge vibrato, vibrations I'd soon do
the Bop to with Bobby Taylor at my first teen party, Pachuco
Hop with my girlfriend Marion in her living room, Twist
with my first husband, Watusi and Swim with my second,
Pony, James Brown, Monkey, Funky Chicken with Jim
Morrison at Whisky á Go-Go in 1966, my future life passing
before my 13-year-old eyes unrecognizable in 1953 in the
back seat of my father's car as he reached to stop the sound,
vibrations irksome noise as his middle age crept and raged and
when my mother, a Modern Millie, said, Ray, don't turn it off,
I like that song, don't be an old fogey, my father harrumphed,
lit up a Lucky Strike and let the radio play on and my life begin.

In 1963

In 1963
I likened myself to Jacqueline Kennedy:
we both had a daughter and son
the same age and we both had lost
our husbands, hers to bullets
and mine to vodka and Vegas.

Although I
wasn't even half as pretty as Jackie Kennedy
I tried to do and say the things
I thought she would do: I never
blew my nose in public, I
wiped only the edges of my
mouth with my napkin while
dining and never put my
elbows on the table. I
read good books and
kept my hair perfectly coiffed.

I taught
my children to name the parts
of their faces in French,
dressed my daughter in good clothes,
showed my son to salute when sad
and regretted not naming him John.

And then
Jackie Kennedy married the Greek magnate,
I married a manic-depressant
and then later that hippie and things
were never again
so nice and neat.

Begin the Beguine

Fourth of July, 1965, his personal
Independence Day, after That Man
left me with three kids, one a baby,
the rent overdue, no milk or bread
in the place, $3 to my name, I lay in bed
all night plotting my suicide like every
woman abandoned there's ever been
not knowing then about Sylvia Plath
not that poetry would've matter.
I planned on gas, too, this: me in
the car in the garage, ignition,
exhaust, sweet dreams, the note
reading: "I can't go on." An hour
before dawn was when I'd do it,
kiss my sleeping kids goodbye, call
their grandmother to come get them
then I'd sneak quietly outside, down
the apartment building stairs so's
not to wake the neighbors (not that
they'd've cared). Appropriately dressed,
my hair combed, I'd even shower and
brush my teeth, the starlight express
of sad night speeding me to begin the
beguine but come the ultramarine of
pre-sunrise, the moonglow of dawn in
my eyes, my tears dried up, a neighbor's
alarm clock went off, someone next door
simmered coffee, birds sang, a cat meowed,
my kids woke up and I wanted to live.
It was only then that I remembered: I
didn't have a car. He'd driven away in it.

Megamorph Ka-pow

I didn't just metamorph
doo-dah diptera
I megamorphed, jumped over, pole-vaulted
from pupa stage to scutterfly
after that man left me with three kids and a fine-toothed comb and I
wearied into that go-go bar wearing my beige wedding suit just like
Doris Day wore in Pillow Talk and I
asked for a go-go girl job because I couldn't take shorthand or type

and all shook up I expected the go-go bar owner to be a leering lech
smoking a Havana cigar who'd ask me to show him my legs
but it was the woman bookkeeper, mother of the bad-ass
bouncer in charge that day who hired me and said I had "class"
didn't even notice my skinny kneecaps
peeking out of my nervous skirt, she viewed
I was a Girl Next Door type with that dorky hairdo
not even mascara on my eyelashes and she told me I didn't have to
wear a French bikini, let it all hang out, unless I wanted to
a leotard was okay and she didn't even see that my hips were too
scrawny to show off anything but pelvic bones

and so I went to work 8 days a week
Good Girl once taught to do what she ought to
pupa housewife who baked cookies, changed diapers
morphed overnight
no cocoon phase into a go-go girl ka-pow
deracinated
but fascinated with all the fluorescent glow and beer flow
and those crazed runaway girls, those poor butterflies
who'd flutterfly-fled rotten stepdads who did bad things in the night
after Mom turned on the light on daughters gone blind
to megamorph into belly-buttoned sexpots in French bikinis
but it took me 2 years to morph brave enough to be seen
baring and bearing red sequins
and by then it was time to megamorph ka-pow again: quantum leap
surpass, bypass my taxonomic rank and specie

to a mightier deracination blast
toward the sky, moon, Mars and stars
and maybe the gods
to become a poet
and a writer.
Oh, my.

Aboard the Bounty

Onto the bar I walked, my first day on the job,
a go-go girl in the raw, onto the bar from the
dressing room where I'd shakily painted my face
with pink and gloss, combed my hair high and
brown, straightened my black stockings smooth,
onto the bar from the dressing room from my
apartment where I'd kissed my kids goodbye,
showed the nanny how to warm the baby's formula,
onto the bar from the dressing room from my
apartment the week after my husband left me
the rent two weeks past due and I looked around
the bar at all the men drinking beer and laughing
and smoking cigars and cigarettes and watching
Robin whose name I didn't know yet dance some
dance I didn't know how to dance yet to the
Rolling Stones singing a song about a Stupid Girl
on the jukebox playing as loud as it would go
and a man wanted me to come here, he wanted
some beer, so I went to him and he pointed up
at Robin, Robin whom I yet did not know, did not
know her stepfather'd raped her, one of her kids'd
been born brain damaged and the drunken man
pointed up at Robin's crotch and asked me, the
first think a drunken man in a go-go bar ever asked me
Is that chick up there on the rag or is she really
a fag with her balls tied up in a jock?

Tales of an Ancient Go-Go Girl

Joan Jobe Smith

Shake, Rattle, Roll and Run á Go-Go

My 5th day on the job, when Bob the Barber
called me bird-legs, I ran off the bar into the
dressing room, shaking, hurrying to put back on
my sundress to cover up my leotard and go home.
I couldn't take it anymore, the cruel, crass remarks,
the drunken maelstrom of men, the stench of
crud, sweat and beer and more beer, beer under
my fingernails, all over my shoes and black
stockings, the smoke in my hair, the pandering
of the drunken men to drink more beer when
they could barely walk or talk so I could make
my $50-quota for the day to make the boss smile
not suspect me of knocking down, the always-
midnight inside the beer bar when the sun
shined bright outside or raindrops fell on the
roof, the claustrophobia of the blood red walls, the
noisy hours of jukebox roaring Rolling Stones,
Ray Charles Shake it up Baby, Wooly Booly,
the fluorescent lights in my eyes while I danced
worrying about falling off the stage, slipping in
the beer-sloppy barroom floor like Sherry did
last week and broke her kneecaps and she may
never walk again and yesterday a new go-go girl
ran screaming from the bar. I only ran. How does
anything take anything, sustain tenacity for life,
survive what it cannot withstand and go on and on?
I was so lonely for my children; I wasn't made for
this strange craziness, I was a fish out of water,
a honeybee upon the tundra. But Robin came in
to tell me Big Red the bouncer had kicked Bob out
made him write me a note: "Sorry. I didn't mean it.
You're a cute kid." So I went back to work as a go-go
girl in the raw. All was forgiven, though not forgotten
even today, 50 years later, I hear the noise, feel my
feet ache, smell the beer as if I pour a keg right now.

Diversified

He wanted to make me a star.
Then why are you looking for one
in a noisy go-go beer bar? I asked him.
"Ah," he said, lighting his big cigar,
"you're cautious. I admire that in a woman."

No, I said, waving cigar smoke
out of my face, I'm cynical, suspicious
and paranoidal.

"Hey," he said, and you got a sense of humor
and irony, real comedienne ability, the next
Carole Lombard or Carol Burnett."

No, I said, pouring his imported bottled beer
into a glass, I'm a hateful witch
hating every minute of my
miserable existence as a go-go girl.

"Wow, a realist. I can just see you now
in an Ingmar Bergman film.
Another Liv Ullman."
He surveyed my façade with his thumb.

And I walked around the bar, sucking in
my stomach, sticking out my chest,
arched my eyebrows like an Audrey Hepburn,
batted my eyes like Lombard looking at Clark
Gable as I surveyed my facade in the huge streaked
wall-to-wall, ceiling-to-floor mirrors
and thought maybe I wasn't so scrawny
after all and when I went to serve 4 pitchers of tap beer
to the pool hustlers at the pool tables, he left,
leaving upon my tip tray one thin dime and a
business card that read:

"Walter B. Somethingorother, Diversified."
No telephone number.
No address.

Purple Hearts

Smitty, the scared shitless Marine (he named
himself) didn't want to go to war he told me
every Sunday afternoon after he drove
his junkheap '54 Ford 60 miles from El Toro Marine
Corps base to Abner's 5 in Long Beach across
the street from the aircraft factory that made the
planes that dropped the bombs on Vietnam
and maybe Smitty someday.

Smitty's best buddy had already gone to Nam
and got blown apart by a land mine Smitty
told me every Sunday afternoon and then
drunk on blood, sweat and Coors he'd play
Bob Dylan on the jukebox
"How does it feel to be on your own…"
over and over and lay his head on the bar
and weep until the pool hustlers shouted
"Hey, play something else goddammit!"

I might've said There, there, to Smitty
and bought him a beer but he hated me
and the other go-go girls, called us
dumb, lazy chicks who didn't know what made
the real world tick: Little Patti who worked
double shifts to support her 4 kids, Linda Lee
who gave all her tips to her old man Reuben who
beat her up whether he was stoned or down
and Robin who ran away at 13 from a sadist stepdad
to earn a living in a stinky go-go beer bar
and not to mention what I was going through
(that included a psycho ex-husband stalking me
but that's another story).

All of us spoils of the eternal war between the
sexes, the languishing war fought in the darkest
love forests and lust jungles. Of course we

were the lucky soldiers, us go-go girls, who'd never
be blown apart by bombs or land mines, eaten to the
bone by Agent Orange and we'd never have to
fear fear itself.

Too bad, though, that on those Sunday afternoons
I grew to hate Smitty, too. I'd liked to have
said, There, there and bought him a beer
and a year later when he came back
from his tour of duty, welcomed him with open arms,
bought him another beer.

But Smitty never came back to Abner's 5
like he said he would to tell us chicks
what was ticking and happening in the real world.
So I knew that Smitty'd either got blown apart
by a bomb or land mine
or fallen in love.

Jehovah Jukebox

The blue collar guys from the aerospace place
across the street from Abner's 5 thought us
go-go girls were damned lucky to work
in a beer bar instead of a hellhole like they did:

we got to do all the things they wanted to
do all day while they pushed and pulled
steel, we got to talk, smoke, shoot pool
or drink a beer anytime we wanted to plus
we got to listen to the jukebox all day long
for free and dance the day away.

Never mind that we'd never get vacation pay,
sick leave, overtime, or old age pensions,
that beer made us fat, the bar's darkness
and smoke made it another kind of hellhole
and that the jukebox was as ear-busting
and mind-numbing as their Jupiter machinery.

Never mind that instead of a crazy,
never-can-be-pleased supervisor
threatening lay-off we had our own
nemesis reminder of our inferiority
and mortality: the Pastor Mick Jagger
fomenting foreboding every day
from the poly-colored plastic jukebox pulpit
as he told us stupid girls, us honky-tonky
women under His thumb, having 19th nervous
breakdowns the ways of the angry-handed
God-of-the-day and screamed at us
that we needed Mother's Little Helpers
that we couldn't get no Satisfaction
or what we want and what a drag it was
getting oh-
old.

Joan Jobe Smith

Jehovah Jukebox

Epidemiology of the Permanent Breast

Brandi Blue wanted big breasts more than anything,
more than money, love, old age or happiness
her own breasts tiny pancakes she taped
to the top of her sequined padded push-up
a joke, a curse, a deformity

so Brandi Blue was happy to pay a plastic surgeon
on Wilshire Boulevard $100 a week
$50 per breast, to shoot into each
an ounce of silicone for 33 weeks
until she was a size 38D

and as her chest grew two perfect Mt. Everests
I longed, too, to see earth bountiful bounce
beneath my chin so one day I went
with Brandi Blue to see her plastic surgeon

saw Brandi Blue lie upon the examining table
naked from the waist up beneath the sheet
as if she waited for a lover man
until finally the doctor entered
carrying a hypodermic syringe the size
of a bayonet he pushed into each naked breast and
pulled out of each naked breast with such magnum force
that Brandi Blue wept from pain until her ears filled with tears
and I looked away, stared up to count the holes in the
acoustical ceiling for many moments while
from each side of her naked breasts
a thin red ribbon of blood streamed down
like the drool of a mammal-hungry, one-fanged vampire
in a very bad dream.

When It Was Fun, It Was Very Very Fun

Some nights it was fun being a go-go girl, usually
on payday and probably when it was a full moon,
the kind of moonglow á go-go moon that makes
everyone inexplicably happy, even Spike our mean
Simon Legree boss was happy because the place was
packed and he was tripping on some good acid and
Rick the machinist was happy, had brought us girls a
5-pound box of Whitman's Sampler and made us
new tiptrays on his machine at work, carved our names
on them, painted them fluorescent to glow beneath the
black lights—our names in lights at last—and Big Dave
and Little Jim were happy, having brought their camera
to take our pictures when Spike wasn't looking and
Dick Dale's surfer guitar was hanging ten, so hot that the
guys and their dates now and then got up to do the Twist
and the bouncers didn't throw them out and the pool hustlers
were happy, winning and tipping for the first time in months
and even Fat Bob tipped two dimes instead of just one
and Suzie Q was getting married instead of having
an abortion and two celebrities wanted to date me
and the three tables of El Toro Marines were BACK
from Nam unwounded and a customer who was cute gave
Brandi Blue a real pearl ring and after I danced football
signals—off-sides, time out, touchdown—to "Mony Mony"
my favorite customer who only came in once a month
gave me $20 and told me I was as funny as Goldie Hawn
and how for sure I would get discovered soon and afterwards
all of us out for breakfast, the guys in the band, Dick Dale,
Spike, we were all still happy and I could afford steak
and eggs and a slice of fresh strawberry pie

and later in bed before sunrise I'd think how fun it all had been
how someday I'd look back on all this and think ....

oh, but then, tomorrow
was another day.

Live: Miss Peggy Lee Singing "Baubles, Bangles and Beads"

Home at last
away from the smoke and noise
of the coal mine, that beer bar
I removed my false eyelashes, fringed bikini and
beer-rotting shoes to bathe, put on my nightgown,
then ate leftover supper fixed by the nanny I paid
to watch my kids 10-hours a day, six days a week

and while my kids slept
in my king-size bed sans husband
pressed together like puppies
waiting for me to come to bed and kiss them

and while the rest of the world spun past:
the Establishment
the Weathermen
the flower children
the Manson murderers
the Vietnam war
the war protesters
the student-shooting National Guards at Kent State
the assassinators of Robert Kennedy and Martin Luther King, Jr
the moon-walking astronauts
the Black Panthers
the Women's Liberation
the Gay Liberation
the Sexual Liberation
the pot smokers, the acid-droppers and vegetarians

I lay on the sofa, sipped a glass of milk
listened to the hi-fi and LPs I bought when 17
Sinatra, Mathis, Nat King Cole, Ivory Joe Hunter
and dreamed about the other man I might've married
who surely would have saved me from All This
oh, that Perfect Other Man, that wondrous god

from the twelfth of never
who would have gotten me under his skin
deep in the heart of him and in the wee small hours of the morning
when he looked at the moon he would've seen
only me.
Unforgettable.
That's what we all are.

The Hippies Were Coming

"...prisoner of your love,
entangled in your web..."
—Tina Turner

The police told me in 1966 I had to
file a report in person so I went to
tell them how after my mean ex-old man
broke my eardrums with his fists and
blacked my eyes till they swelled shut
and he started calling me all hours of the
night calling himself the Big Hammer
and telling me how he was going to make
me his Little Nail, how he waited for me
after work to see if I went home with
any guys, how one midnight he banged
on my door, looked at me with crazy
eyes and made me fry bacon as if we
were still married and another night
he chased me out my door to the alley
during a full moon, a wolf chasing a
rabbit, to my VW and when I jumped in
and drove off he jumped on and tried
to eat me through the windshield and I
asked the police what I should do
where could I get a gun to protect
me and my kids but the police noticed
I was young and a little bit pretty so they
asked me if I had a lover and I said
no but they didn't believe me, they
guffawed and Dirty Harry-tough told me
that if I got me a gun and shot my ex-
old man they'd have to come arrest me
and put me in prison for premeditation
because they had it all—and they pointed
down at it—written down in this report.

Soon the Hippies would be coming
and name them Pigs.

O, Jim, look up there, in the air

on that building across from Fingerprints there
on 4th Street in Long Beach, California—June, 2016:
it's YOU, Jim Morrison, from 1967, flying in the stucco sky
jet-plane, propelled by a mysterious mojo-rising
a levitating Oracle breaking on through
to the other side as you, Jim, in that old Jim Coke photo,
sing, scream, and zing and zap in that microphone so long ago.

I didn't like you back then, Jim, in 1967,
nagging me to light your fire. I wanted heaven
with Elvis loving me tender, wanting me, needing me,
Tony Bennett wooing me with his When Joanna Loved Me
Frank Sinatra longing for me because he got me
under his skin but you, Jim, you called me an L.A. Woman
so alone, so alone, my hair burning, told me about heartache
and the loss of god, how faces look ugly
when you're strange. Was I strange, Jim, back then? Yes, and Why:
I was a go-go girl when all the good women were housewives
baked cookies for their babies on their Sears Kenmore gas ranges
while I, one in 5, tried to get out alive
with killers on the road with brains squirming like toads
because that no-good man had done left me with nothing but a
fine-tooth comb and no milk in the refrigerator, the rent due.

O, Jim, you were no hanky-panky Frankie, no, no.
Nor did you leave your heart in my San Francisco
but you never called me a Hound Dog, didn't think me cruel
so I forgive you now, Jim, in 2016, 50 years later
as I watch you, Flying Jim Morrison, up there in the air, breaking
on through to the other side where death makes angels of us all,
finally breaking through to me because I'm old and grown up now
and can take it now, Jim, take it how you told me The Truth, not lies—
my very own write-on, right-on Mr. Mojo Rising.

Feminist Arm Candy for the Mafia and Frank Sinatra

Go-go girl Sindy, who changed the first letter of her name
from "C" to "S" for obvious reasons, said us go-go girls
at the Playgirl Club in 1969 were nothing but waitresses
in bikinis, dancing workhorses, indentured servitude (she
forgot to mention how much money we made, more than
tenured Cal Tech profs, aerospace executive engineers, we
drove new cars, dressed groovy as Cher, had cuter boyfriends,
guys in the band were *our* groupies). So Sindy decided to
organize a Go-Go Girl Union, make our millionaire bosses
give us lunchtime, sick leave, retirement funds, vacation pay,
overtime for that hour extra we worked cleaning up the place
while our mean boss Spike called us lazy tramps. Sindy went
to the California state labor board, ACLU, wrote letters to our
Congressman detailing us go-go girls's "UNendowment of
inalienable Rights" promised us in the U.S. Constitution and
when the bosses told her Shut up, get back to work, one night
she shing-a-linged, right in the middle of Dick Dale's famous
showstopper solo, Sindy jumped off the stage, pulled the plug
on Dick Dale's electric guitar—rrrip!—as off she went to Vegas
for some fun in the sun, be a showgirl at the Stardust or Flamingo,
find a millionaire to marry and 6 months later when she returned
to hello-goodbye-again, 20 pounds thinner, hair bleached white
dried-up Monet haystack, eyes swollen from a day-ago beating,
nostrils cracked from snorting cocaine, eyeballs red from day-
time pot smoking and a slipped disc because they'd made her
wear 50-pound headpieces, work 8 days a week plus matinees
and be arm candy after hours for the Mafia and Frank Sinatra,
she warned us: "Stay the hell away from Vegas, baby, the men
are very BAD there." Then Sindy walked out, the first feminist
go-go girl, off again this time for Chicago, her name changed
to Windy as in bad weather blowing in. What Windy would do
there in the Windy City of Chicago to make the world right for us
go-go girls and women everywhere to find Life, Liberty and the
Pursuit of Happiness in turn-on, tune-out 1969, God only knew.

Aretha Franklin, Baby, with Respect

Aretha Franklin, baby, am remembering you When.
Not that When when you wore that big hat at Obama's
Inauguration but the When of August, 1966, year after
the Watts Riots when I met you at that blacks-only club
on Crenshaw in Watts weeks before your "Respect" aired
all over the radio and got you rich, famous and respected.
They didn't know why white chick me was in the club,
that I'd been dumped by my sexpot go-go girlfriend
Linda Alura who'd taken off with her Black Panther
lover and I didn't even drink, just sat there on the floor
on those crash pillows, snapping my white chick fingers
to the soul sound beat as you, Aretha Franklin, baby,
sang your R-E-S-P-E-C-T spelling it the way it should be
loud and clear while that groovy black dude taught me
how to Boogaloo, Shingaling, Jerk and Temptation Walk.
Oh, baby, what a rough 1966 I had while you moved on
to a great future. My 1967 wasn't much better so when I
auditioned at the Condor Room up in North Beach, I
picked on the jukebox for irony and good luck your new
hit song Respect, just a little bit of respect I wanted, too,
in those days when just a gaudy go-go girl. I got the job
but turned it down, too scared to go topless, so came back
to L.A. go-go. And now, Aretha Franklin, baby, you're
not doing well; news of your illness got me remembering
you, though you'll never know how much I respect you,
remember every day your soul sound real and wise, your
black woman big heart, your finger-snappy upbeat always
got me going when it was my turn to dance, even when I
didn't want to—but always remembering how to spell
R-E-S-P-E-C-T right and proud when no one else did.

Vice

Even though in 1969 when in L.A. strippers
and topless dancers bumped and grinded
the night away, vice officers began to arrest
the go-go girls in Long Beach, the city leaders
deciding that go-go girls dancing the Monkey,
the Twist, the Mashed Potato and the Funky
Chicken were lewd and obscene
so plainclothes vice officers sat in the go-go bars
day and night drinking beer, pretending to leer
as they waited for us go-go girls to dance
and then the vice officer would flash his badge
help us off the stage and slap handcuffs on us
while the go-go bar jukebox played on without us
and oh, how those vice officers must've
got their kicks driving us ratted-haired
tarantula-false-eyelashed, sequin-bikini'd girls
down Long Beach streets to the police station
stopping at red lights while law-abiding citizens
stared at the captured criminals in the back seat
of the plainclothes vice officer cop car
because I know the go-go girls sure got a kick out of it
and the cop whistles while they were booked,
mug-shot and bailed out of jail because the girls
always came back to work bragging and laughing
about their Criminal Record for their heinous crimes:
dancing the Monkey, the Twist, the Mashed Potato
and the Funky Chicken: Obscenities! those goofy
dances, names of which decades later would sound silly
like the names of children's games and toys and
back then I was too young and a bit stupid to realize
the absurdity of it all, the yin and yang of cosmic idiocy
of what's good, what's evil until one day when I
was almost age 50 it would all make sense
the absolute Truth of it:
that Time always marches on
without making one bit of sense at the time.

Right as Rain

When my father found out about
me being a go-go dancer
he turned red as sunburn and nearly
died young then instead of a year later.
A juke-joint dive! he yelled when I got home
him and my mother coming down to Long Beach
from Sacramento surprising me, catching me
in the worst act of my life.
It's a nice place, I explained.
A honky-tonk hellhole! he yelled,
his Texas drawl as baritonal
as tornado, him grinding his teeth
and chain-smoking Lucky Strikes.
The guys are nice, I explained,
aerospace executives, Vietnam vets,
businessmen, Cal State grad students, sometimes
movie stars and famous astronauts.
Drunkards! he yelled.
But I'm a go-go girl, I bragged.
You're a fringed floozy! he yelled,
the prodigal jazz dancer's pedant papa
a vox savant of morality, a Newton
holding a wormy apple, a van
Leeuwenhock eyeing grandiose beasties
so I didn't explain that I did it
because I made more money in one week
than he did in three.
I'd soon quit dancing for other reasons
but right then he was right as rain because
he was my father.

The Carol Burnett Show

After my father died and I had to
drop out of college for the second time
to go back to work as a go-go girl again,
my mother came to live with me to take
care of my 3 kids even though she didn't
approve one bit of what I did for a living,
said I was just goofing off and having a
good time as a go-go girl dancing all night
even though I told her I wasn't having fun
and so ashamed was she of me she lied to my
grandmothers, told them I was a dancer on
the Carol Burnett Show on tv and that's why
I worked nights, wore mini-skirts and false
eyelashes but my mother told her sister Vera,
a divorcee like me, the truth and when Vera
came to visit from Colorado, the two of them
came to see me at the Playgirl Club and Spike
my boss gave them a front row table and a free
pitcher of beer and 2 free bags of potato chips
and there they sat, wearing white gloves and
Jackie Kennedy pillbox hats, Kleenexes from
their purses for napkins on their laps as they
sipped ladylike their beer as they watched us
go-go girls dance, sling pitchers, kegs, tanks
of beer to the drunken aerospace execs, the
construction workers, surfers, Nam-bound
Marines, watched us empty ashtrays, dance,
wash beer glasses, dance, sweep up broken
glass after some pool hustlers got into a fight
and dance and the next day at noon as I sat in
my kitchen nibbling my bowl of cold cereal,
somnolistic-zombie and achy from working
till 3 a.m., I heard my mother outside yelling
at the trash men not to make so much noise
banging trashcans, they might wake up her
daughter who worked nights and her daughter
worked DAMNED HARD to earn a living!
One of the nicest things my mother ever said
about me and I can finally appreciate it today,
decades later, now that I'm all rested up.

Dancing in the Frying Pan

Richard, my go-go agent was always calling me about my
go-go girl gigs from some pay phone off some L.A. highway
or freeway while trucks, motorcycles, cars roared by as he
yelled into the telephone receiver at me: "HEY, BABY!" he
yelled the last time he called me. "I can't book you no more
at no more places! NO PLACE WANTS YOU BACK!" (ROAR)
"Joe's Bar & Grill in Pomona says you're a shitty dancer! No more!
Joe says you kicked over some Mexican dudes' beer!" (ROAR)

"They were grabbing at my ankles..."

"And the Blue Bunny says no more go-go Joanie! All the guys
walked out when you came on!" (ROAR)

"I came on after that 6-foot-tall 50-inch-boobed showgirl..."

"And the Amber Inn says all you could dance was the bossa nova
and jitterbug!" (ROAR)

"The old guys kept playing Sinatra and Glenn Miller and Brubeck
and Tony Bennett on the jukebox."

"And the Shimmy Shack said you blew your nose all the time and
coughed and sneezed..." (ROAR)

"I caught a cold from my kids..."

"EXCUSES! EXCUSES!" Richard roared inside the telephone booth
and while some truck, motorcycle or car backfired and a cop car siren
squealed by, Richard—even though he personally thought me okay and
cute—fired me (ROAR) from a job I never wanted in the first place,
a job that had caused me to break out in hives that glowed like
bloodshot eyeballs beneath the fluorescent lights at the go-go bars
and for the rest of the Summer of Love, 1967 I lay in the L.A. sun
8 hours a day dreaming about my future until my tan peeled off
and leaves on the trees began to fall—stupid me never dreaming
for one minute that working for Richard's Rich Street Freelance
Dance Agency would NOT be the rottenest job I'd ever have.

Sergeant Pepper's Lonely Hearts Club Band

It's hard to believe today how bellybuttons
once drove men crazy in 1965, bellybuttons
the raison d'etre, Original Sin of go-go bars
when French bikinis were still banned on
California state beaches and American tv
and I wouldn't wear a bikini at first, I just
wore leotards or costumes showing just a bit
of midriff, the go-go bar owners not caring,
a shy new go-go girl gave the place class, but it
drove the guys crazy, one guy one day offering me
$20 to show him my bellybutton and I told him
No, I don't have one, but he didn't believe me.
I'm a Martian, I told him, but he didn't believe
that either, he just got drunker and drunker
and yelled at me all afternoon, Hey, Baby,
lemme see yer bellybutton Baby but I kept on saying
No.

It's all so silly nowadays.

I sure could've used that $20 back then in 1965.

I still could.

Painting the Topless Dancer till We Glowed

Maida the topless dancer lay naked on her
motel bed smoking marijuana and giggling,
ticklish, while my hippie boyfriend and I
painted yellow fluorescent daisies and green
fluorescent vines and leaves up and down and
around her breasts, arms, butt, back and thighs
and then we painted orange fluorescent butterflies
on her shoulders, nipples, belly button and knees
and then, my idea, we painted all over her bod
purple, blue and white fluorescent dots
I told Maida to tell the guys who would watch
her dance at the topless go-go bar was "rainbow rain"
drunk guys sometimes liking a little poetry
and Maida did and she was so popular that night
with all that beautiful fluorescent paint all over her
while she danced and glowed at her topless dancing job
she made $200 in tips plus another $100 when a
good-looking guy paid her to let him come
home with her to her motel to watch her
wash off the fluorescent paint and he wound up
loving her so much he bought her a house where they
still live today and later that night because my
hippie boyfriend and I'd had so much fun
laughing and painting till we glowed like Maida
he asked me to marry him and even though
I deep-down knew that he'd never amount to anything
with all that fluorescence on his mind,
two weeks later I did. It's really amazing how
a coat of paint can change how
everything really is.

Out of Sight

To teach my out of sight hippie huz a thing or 2
for staying away 2 days and nights at a Love In, I
took all his hippie clothes: his purple tie-dyed bell-
bottoms, his ratty rabbit fur vest, orange-magenta
madras cloth meditation p.j.'s, marijuana-leaf print
tank top and Jim Morrison black leather pants and I
played tug of war with our dog, a Doberman pinscher
whose sharp killer-shark teeth ripped them to shreds
the way we thought she'd do some day to a cat burglar
while I cooed: "Atta girl, atta girl, good dog, good dog."
Then I got all my hippie huz's beloved hippie albums:
LP's of the Beatles, The White Album, Rubber Soul,
3-Dog Night, Vanilla Fudge, Donovan, Rolling Stones,
Bob Dylan, The Doors, The Animals, Big Brother and
the Holding Company, Cream, Credence Clearwater,
Led Zeppelin, Steppenwolf, Canned Heat, Jefferson
Airplane, Country Joe and the Fish and I placed all
those licorice pizzas step-stones on the stairs leading
up to our bedroom while my good dog watched from
below until I called: "Here, girl, come to Mommy—"
and up, up she came, slipping, sliding but sure-foot
happy dog scratching zebra-stripes all over all those
hippie albums. "Good girl," I praised, "Out of sight!"
Later that night when hippie huz finally came home
sunburned, red-eyed from doing his own thing and
letting it all hang out at love ins and saw the mess,
"MY GOD!" he exclaimed and asked. "WHAT THE
HELL HAPPENED?" and I answered: I didn't do it.

Poem from the Los Angeles County Gaol, 1970

Yes, I was innocent, hippie husband had done it.
But I went to jail anyway, innocent just like those
other women there bamboozled by some man:
the young bleached blonde from Utah who'd
snuck out her bedroom window to date that bad
boy her father hated and rode passenger in his
stolen car run-away all the way to California;
the middle-aged lady facing 10 counts of Murder
One for performing abortions for money to pay
her husband's gambling debts because the bookies
were going to chop off his legs; the grey-haired
widow who sat on her jail cot hands folded
school girl ashamed for shoplifting to get by
after her husband of 40 years suddenly died
leaving her bereaving and broke; all of them
women just like me, you or your mother with
ovaries, eyebrows, toes, women with over-the-
rainbow dreams, oh, and those 20 biker chicks
busted with their biker old men after holding an
entire town hostage for a weekend of brawl and
the next morning the biker chicks when we all
put back on our own clothes to go for court
arraignment were angry when they saw their
clothes had been laundered. Dammit! said the
one who liked to have the most fun riding on the
back of a Harley, holding tight onto her tough
leathered biker old man's chest and thought fun
is wind blowing in her hair and something hard
between her legs (and maybe it is). Goddammit!
she said, they washed away all my old man's
pecker tracks on my jeans. Do any of you know
how long it took us to make my jeans all streaked
and striped groovy like that? I did not want to know.
I was innocent.

The Treasure of the Sierra Madre

Listening to Led Zeppelin, my dope-dealing
hippie huz and his bro's used to snort when
they laughed so hard snorting cocaine while
they bagged whites, lidded kilos of pot and
capped THC all night. Daytime, wearing their
long hair, tie-dyes and roach clips like "Kick Me"
signs, they toughed up their biceps and buttocks
in go-go beer bars boogalooing, shooting pool,
pouring beer pitchers and arm wrestling while
they scored with the guys and go-go girls.
They bragged about being retired when
asked what they did for a living dressed
like that and they almost did retire at age 30
on the Big Scam except that a Riverside farmer
spotted the Cessna loaded with Mexican hashish
landing in his north 40 at midnight. Hannifin
jumped bail and split town. Charlie Brown got
snuffed. Dirty Dave turned state's and skated.
Jerry got Soledad and my huz the honor farm.
Come 20 years later, all the dudes they used
to call squares, lame, out of it, the firemen,
the postmen, the narcs, were all retiring with
a nice pension while huz and his bro's, then
calling themselves Party Animals, drank beer,
wore baseball caps turned backwards while
watching sports in sports bars and during
half-times they talk, without snorting with
laugher or coke about how good—jeez, and
cheap—good dope used to be and what they
would've done with all that Scam Money and
looked for work they could do with a hangover—
their biceps and buttocks gone flat and flimsy
from all that humping of The Establishment.

Getting Drunk with My Third Mother-In-Law

She laughs like a madam might
having finally found herself
a thousand-dollar john.
She's the only woman I know
who can outdrink me and she
likes me to make hers half vodka
half juice, then two-thirds vodka
a third juice, then she winks, we
drink, communal beasts at the same
watering hole, nothing else mattering.

My first mother-in-law nagged me
for not diapering the baby often enough
my second one didn't like me knowing
that I wasn't a virgin but my third one
just wants to laugh and have a good time.

Once the two of us, alone on barstools
drinking gin, she told me her first husband
walked out on her, the second one beat her
and I told her my second one beat me, too
tried to kill me with his bare hands
and my third mother-in-law
looked me straight in the eye
for the first and last time
and told the bartender to bring two more

and not so much juice this time.

The Postman Always Rings Twice

I'm running away with John Garfield today
right after he gets my fat old husband drunk
stuffs him into the trunk of that 1936 black LaSalle
and shoves it and him over the cliffs
exploding into the ocean and on the rocks
the way John Garfield's and my toothy kisses do.
But I'll have to talk John Garfield into doing it.
He was a good old Joe until he met me and became
a fall guy falling for my midriff and bleached blonde
hair and he'll try to resist, scream "Cora!
They HANG YA for doing things like that!"
And I'll scream right back: "But I wanna BE
somebody I don't wanna be named SMITH
all my life and sling hash all my life
I want bus rides white shoe polish and a string of
REAL PEARLS!" And John Garfield
will slap me to bring me back to my senses
but then just to make me happy and smile again
he'll kill my drunk fat old husband
and we'll collect the double indemnity
settle down and buy a new black LaSalle
a lemon grove in San Diego
I'll learn to fry chicken Texas-style
John Garfield will buy me some REAL pearl
EARRINGS!!
disappointed
I'll yearn for white bread and mayonnaise
my midriff will turn to scrambled eggs my
milk white hair to mud
John Garfield'll start drinking beer and get a fat gut
we'll be childless
he'll start pinching the neighbors' daughters' butts
and one night
while John Garfield snores in our brass bed
I'll get me out the frying pan the big iron one
I fry chicken Texas-style in and I'll
bash John Garfield's brains out all over his feather pillow.

That's what I should've done in the first place.

74

Too Sexy for Clothes @ Cal State U Long Beach, 1973

Everyone was crazy in 1973, streaking everywhere
taking their clothes off and going naked at love-ins,
sometimes across the stage at the Academy Awards
and every Friday at Cal State U Long Beach students
streaked across campus, one day the Science Majors:
Einstein, Isaac Newton, Pierre and Marie Curie, Louis
Pasteur, a slide rule dangling from his groin and the
next week the naked Art Majors: Monet, Picasso,
Michelangelo, Georgia O'Keefe, van Gogh with
amber sunflowers painted all over his pink bod
while the rest of the students who wore clothes sat
on the grass watching, applauding and smoking pot
and some of the professors were too sexy for their
clothes, too, dated their young students, an A for a lay

and my T.S. Eliot seminar prof one day unzipped his
fly to let it all hang out for my eyes only as I sat in
front of his lecture table as he explicated to the class
"Ash Wednesday." I'd never seen anything like it, age
33. I'd been a go-go girl for 7 years. I'd come back to
college for knowledge, literally clean up my act, also
learn sense and sensibility, to be or not to be. Not be
too sexy for my clothes, learn to streak naked. And then
one awful day that 19-year-old wannabe-Rimbaud in
my poetry writing class organized for next Friday a
Poet Streaking Party: all us poets to meet at the rest
rooms in the student union to take off all our clothes.

Then, all us Emily Dickinsons, Sylvia Plaths, Rod Mc
Kuens, T.S. Eliots, Walt Whitmans and e e cummings
amongst us were to run naked together down the stairs
to the bookstore, then run naked past the grassy area,
then to the English Department to run naked up and
down the stairs. "It'll be a blast! Out of sight!" said
Rimbaud. But none of us poets showed up. So come
Monday our Poetry Prof Dr. Lee thanked us all for not

streaking, praised us for being dignified English Majors
and then chuckled impishly as he held up a new book by
a new writer Charles Bukowski: *Erections, Ejaculations,
Exhibitions and General Tales of Ordinary Madness.*
For sale at CSULB's bookstore. Roll over, Jane Austin.
Bob Dylan, too, because times were a'changin' again.

Bukowski Chugs Cheap Beer @ the No-No á Go-Go

Bukowski laughed har har har when I told him I'd
been a go-go girl for 7 years, the bad luck time for
breaking a mirror, minimum sentence for a felony
conviction. In 1973 Bukowski'd thought me one of
those feminists who wanted to kick his ass, booed,
stomped en masse out of his poetry readings. Worse,
he'd thought me another bored housewife going back to
college, my hard working schmuck hubby buying my
books, tuition and bellbottoms, cooking his own supper,
diapering the baby while I read Sexton, Plath and Jong
and flirted with cute professors. Bukowski never drank
at any of those go-go bars I worked those 7 years. Too
expensive, too uppity and all that rock 'n' roll too noisy.
No, he preferred the basso nova and cheap beer at the
No-No á Go-Go's where barmaids wore overalls, not
fringed bikinis and could toss out any drunk, including
him, with one bare hand. Midnights Buk phoned me long
distance, drunk because his Woman had left him again,
he listened intently to my go-go girl tales about men like
him, broke, lonely who drank too much, said wild things,
talk of men not like him: astronauts, murderers, rich men
wearing diamond pinky rings while Bukowski chugged his
cheap beer in his cheap apartment in L.A., blew smoke
from cheap cigars into the telephone at me sipping cheap
white wine 40 miles away till one night Bukowski finally
said: You gotta write about all that madness, Kid. So I did.

Beer Can in the Garden

After the poetry reading, Bukowski was
supposed to go to a Tea in his honor, yes,

a Tea, and cookies, for Bukowski, sponsored by
the good people of the nearby First Assimilationist
Church, no, no booze, the good church people
probably thinking his Henry Chinaski persona
mere fiction and I drove him there in my white

Volkswagen Bug, the Laguna Beach aquamarine sky
matched the horizon high-sea and sunshine sizzled
above the church steeple dazzling the birds of
paradise in full-bloom August smiles, wearing
their best party hats and when Bukowski
saw all the good church people standing on the
neatly mowed green-green lawn, saw the men

in their good Sunday suits, the women in
their pinkest frocks, waiting, watching for
his arrival, he told me, Don't stop, keep going,
I need a beer, so I drove him to the nearest
liquor store where he bought a 12-pack, snapped
open a can and told me, Get me the hell outa here

so I drove him to my old go-go girlfriend
Suzi Q's house in a bad part of Santa Ana and
Bukowski was glad to meet her and her
boyfriend Brucie, shook their hands, flirted
with Suzi Q and while she fixed us spaghetti

and garlic bread and Chianti and we ate and talked
all night, Bukowski made us laugh until 4
in the morning when Linda, the First Linda,
drove him back home to L.A. and I didn't see

Bukowski again for nearly a year and the good, tea-
sipping, cookie-munching people of the First
Assimilationist Church didn't see Bukowski again

ever.

Charles

BukOwski

Epic *GLOTTIS*:

His Art & His Women (& me)

Joan Jobe Smith

BUKOWSKI

REVIEW 4

MEN'S LIB. POSTER.

BUK

No Leonardo da Vinci Mona Lisa

Bukowski drew my portrait, me as a
buxom giantess with wild hairy Medusa
hair smoking a cigarette, himself as a six-inch man
smoking a cigarette, too, looking up my skirt
hiked high showing a garter belt and a lot
of leg (Bukowski was a leg man) and
he named this inky cartoon stained with
beer "Men's Lib Poster."

How do ya like it, Kid?

Well, it's no Mona Lisa. Maybe a Moaning
Lisa.

Why's that?

I don't smoke, Bukowski.

Well, you should smoke

you'd look sexy if you smoked.

Oh, Henry

Bukowski told me the reason he chose
Charles for his writer name instead of
Henry his real first name was because
he didn't think Henry was a very writerly
name and I, a full-of-myself undergrad said
But what about Henry James, Henry Miller,
Ibsen, O. Henry? And Bukowski laughed
letting me know he was glad to know that
I wasn't the bimbo he thought I was
and I laughed, glad he didn't think me
a bimbo and he laughed some more
harder, his eyes twinkling, letting me
know it wasn't so much knowledge he had
but psychic insight that he could see
right through me and it was scarier than hell
to know that someone knew you so well.

Eggs Overeasy

I was frying eggs overeasy when
I heard Bukowski had died and
suddenly the yolks came alive,
grew to the size of heavyweight
Golden Gloves smashing my spatula
and jaw while the kitchen swelled
shut around me like a big, blackened
eye. Bukowski's obit was in the Thursday
newspaper, my favorite paper of the
week for the Food Section, the recipes
(this week sickening ones of what to
do with peanuts), the supermarket ads
(this week St. Pat's Day specials,
corned beef for 89 cents a pound,
cabbage for nine, rye $1.69 he'll
never eat again, if he ever did,
or the wine I later drink with my
husband who mourns more than me
as he listens to a Bukowski Live tape
and reads over and over the only letter
Hank ever wrote him. Hank never knew
was too busy to care, that his life
changed ours, that we'd come to know
his mojo poetry as well as the backs
of our hearts where manna and mortality
are stored. We'd wanted him to
live to be 400, after all, he was 200
at age 30, he was supposed to keep telling
it like it is forever, be our Poet Man,
nexus and code breaker of nether worlds.
But no one dies when you want
him or her to, death seldom an Ides
of March or hemlock time for which
you can set your alarm clock as, as he

was quoted in his obit: You carry in
one hand a bundle of darkness that
accumulates each day. The eggs
overeasy were the coldest I ever ate,
a March ninth wind blowing in through
the window turning them to ice).

Joan Jobe Smith, March 9, 1994

Bereaving Bukowski, March 10, 2016

Oh, dear, Bukowski, so sorry I forgot
yesterday to bereave and commemorate the
22nd anniversary of your March 9, 1994
demise but I got too busy being happy
celebrating Piscean birthdays of my two
beautiful granddaughters Camille and
Nastassia and my dear friend Anne's sister
Margrit's and 5 fine poets and my special
old pal, father of Pearl David and his twin
brother Dennis's and then I got too caught
up in the mundane to mourn you while I

cooked a big pot of Beans and Garlic, one
of your favorite meals I fixed you in 1975, I
got busy skimming the scum and stirring
the big pot of deep ruddy-brown pintos till
tender, then chopped carrots to pretty it up
and sweeten the beans a bit and then later
the world was too much with me to talk to
my better angels about you, ask how you are,
did the gods get you a typer out there? when
we watched the Presidential Candidates
debate on tv. Hank, you'd like Hillary, I think;
you liked wise women; but I think you'd like
Bernie Sanders more, your fellow Pole who
comes out fighting, just like you, quick with
the punches, no rope-a-doping and I think

you'd like all this modern techno stuff: email,
Facebook, Twitter, selfies and Googling Charles
Bukowski but I'm sure you'd hate the bad stuff,
the closing of bookstores and Hollywood Park
and all the homeless, loss of jobs, fracking
and global warming, L.A. temps the highest
ever recorded in California history. But then
again, maybe you'd love it; you loved the sun.

Oh, Bukowski, who knows what you'd love
about Now. You are a paradox, always North
of No South, Drowning in Flame, Burning in
Water. You were a Leo Sun-Virgo Rising, a
wild lion yet a cool cat, tough yet tender, smart
ass yet a sweetheart and how I miss your wit
and grit and wondrous words. I miss you like
dinner, my kitten that got lost in the rain, my
white chiffon prom dress, the polar icecaps,
silver dollars and the black rhinoceros and
yesterday marked the 22nd year of that sad
day you went away forever. Je t'aime, mon cher
Bukowski. Rest in peace, caprice and expertise.

Alley-Walker

*after Bukowski performed for last time
at the Hollywood Troubador, 1976*

walking down the alley
looking for you the black man
standing in a back alley doorway
eyeballed me
I could tell he wondered why the hell
I walked down the pitch black alley
like I owned it kicked a beer can
like some hooker who walks the streets
around the corner of Western Avenue
a Hooker Row where L.A. ladies of the eve
wearing sequined T-shirts
open-toed wedgies walk slow and easy
as if the wind blows their asses side to side
they way it does palm trees
he probably thought I was on my way to roll
some John behind the garbage cans
and stuff his empty wallet into a dumpster
but I was looking for you
thought you'd run out on me at the Troubador
after Bukowski read his last poem
took off in your green Mustang
leaving me there to pay for all that champagne
not a dime in my tote bag
to call a cab or friend
you bastard I said as I walked through the back door
of the Troubador
even the bouncer afraid to ask if I had a ticket
walked past the booths and barstools
the men's rest room to the bar
where you sat drinking our champagne
"Jesus Christ, baby, I've been looking
all over for you
Where the hell have you been?"

Twenty-Ninth Day

Just when I can beat him forty-love
smack a grand-slam bottom of the ninth
swim the English Channel in a snowstorm
quote epic-glottal verbatim from the Wall Street Journal
Shakespeare
and Nietzsche
and the Oxford Unabridged Dictionary
and start thinking I could piss standing up
if I tried
it comes
this outrageous error
like a period flopped prone in the middle
of an incomplete sentence
suddenly
kicking me in the gut
a balking jackass
while the fat lady moon laughs
her ermine iridescence
and turns an about-face
a psychotic bystander
leaving the scene of the accident.

Fistful of Dandelion Cha Cha Cha

Couldn't wait to grow up, wear Claudette Colbert
Liz Taylor, Audrey Hepburn black slinky cocktail clothes,
go to piano bars, sip martinis, request As Time Goes
By, dance in the dark cheek to cheek till the wee small
hours of the morning with my heartthrob tuxedo'd date
named Cary, Rock or Marcello who'd give me dew-kissed
gardenias and whisper Moonlight becomes you, it goes
with your hair. But by the time Time went by, times had
been a'changin', the Beatles had arrived with tickets to
ride eight days a week doing it in the road. The Stones
couldn't get no satisfaction, piano bars became stages
for topless dancers while my tie-dye'd, peace-sign'd
dates named T.J., Big Don and Dakota Dave gave me
fistfuls of dandelions, passed joints and tequila bottles
at love-ins, made me parched LSD-corroded promises
to light my fie-yarr. And as the changing times went on
I bought black cocktail dresses anyway, first a sleek but
sweet Lanz, then a sequined Saks 5th Avenue, a Donna
Karan v-neck cut sexy to the waist, a strapless Spanish
lace ankle-length, a mutton-sleeve Laura Ashley velvet
just like Princess Di's and then, in the hard times of the
2-thousand-oughts, I bought for $29 a thrift store 1951
Lili Taylor satin sheath waltz-length with chiffon peplum
and bodice and cape, sartorial votives of hope unworn in
my closet, good as new cocktail dresses all ready, set to
go mambo, cha cha cha, foxtrot or even do a boogaloo
perchance Cary, Rock or Marcello finally calls, tell me at
long last that Moonlight becomes me, goes with my hair.

George Harrison (1943-2001)

Though I scoffed at Beatlemania in 1964, thought
the Fabulous Four ludicrous, off-key and not fab
at all, when the girls in the office played the game
Name Your Favorite Beatle I picked George the
way I'd've picked eenie instead of meenie, minie
or moe. Those bad-boyish, long-haired Beatles
composed music for the Nowhere men of my
generation, provided them *raison d'être, cause
célèbre* to stop growing up, get a job, haircuts,
go to war, get married. Mop-topped Peter Pans
day tripping with Eleanor Rigby, garage bands
and jabberwocky cool, they let it be, did it in the
road in yellow submarines, nothing to get hung
about while I was the walrus, Lady Madonna so
tired ob-la-di 8 days a week helter skelter back in
the USSR, HELP! rearing 3 kids in strawberry
fields seeming forever all those decades when not
one time did I have time to think of my Favorite
Beatle George or that I had one until last week
when George died and suddenly I realized what a
hangdog dowdy I'd been and how that New Years
Eve night I watched my no-good hippie husband
dancing in the dark at the party with that pretty
airline stewardess to George's "Something" and
then take her outside in the moonlight where they
kissed on the lips, George was standing there in the
shadows of the starry night only waiting for this
moment to arise to whisper to me: Here comes the
sun. Baby, you can drive my car. Oooh, you were
meant to be near me. Take a sad song and make it
better and when I did, George held my hand in the
octopus's garden 'coz something in the way I moved
attracted George Harrison like no other lover.

Go-Go Girl Reunion

Those who don't show up at Reunions either
think they're too good or have something to hide.
So since go-go girls once let it all hang out of bikinis
and can claim neither that vice nor the virtue, we all
showed up at the Playgirl Club where 10 years before
we'd all slung beer and shook our tail feathers till 2 a.m.
Jenny the most beautiful and best dancer of all was there
wearing pink shantung and a sable, the only one of us
to marry a millionaire although we all tried and Jodi
showed up, now thinner and a reborn Christian; Tiara,
too, in spite of warrants for her arrest. Barbie was still
a barmaid but now lived with a younger, better-shooting
pool hustler; Linda Lee just bought a new Mercedes, a
nose job and boob job all paid for by one of her old sugar
daddies. And Dee-Dee, wearing thick glasses, her eyes
having gone bad from too much LSD, had kicked drugs
and now drank nothing but Jack Daniels on the rocks.
Betty had given up macramé and now taught aerobics.
Suzi Q got a broker's license and was getting rich quick
on commercial real estate; Cher—not the real one—just got
her PhD in Psychology from Prestigious U and said she'd
seen more weirdoes and crazies when she was at the Playgirl
than she ever saw in a Psycho ward. The new Playgirl owner
Dick Dale had his band play "Night Train" and all us old go-
go girls drunk enough got up on the stage, raised skirts above
our knees and wiggled around while Dick Dale took Polaroids
and said over the microphone to the audience and us that us
go-go girls weren't getting older we were only getting better
and above the whistles, hoots and applause, I heard one of
his 20something cocktail waitress laugh to a co-worker and
say: "*Yeah, sure,*" knowing, certain that she would never
show up to any reunion of any kind. Wizened with young,
she thought she knew how to hold back sunsets with her tongue.

Whiskey á Go-Go Slow-Mo with Jim Morrison

Whisky á Go-Go in 1965 packed in the sin and in crowd,
Brando, Warhol, Frank and Mia, me high in the corner cage
smoke in my eyes auditioning to the new band The Doors.
Stupid name said another go-go girl, lead singer always stoned
LSD-corroded croaking "Light my fie-yarrr" over and over
till blisters on our dancing feet began to bleed and we got so
tired we had to dance boogaloo slo-mo so I turned down the
Whiskey job, walked to my car through Sunset Strip, Sonny
and Cher look-alikes, runaway girls, panhandling hippies,
stalled traffic and worried cops, turned right to find my VW
parked up a Hollywood hill a mile away. I cared not about this
hipster counterculture, the yeah-yeah generation outa sight cool
cats screaming Bummer, man! when narcs busted them for
possession and vagrancy or worse. Went to work at The Fort
a beer bottle's throw from the L.A. Harbor and oil refineries
packed with the workingstiff sin and in crowd, stevedores, crazy
bikers, sailors, machinists who dive bombed into beer pitchers 8
days a week and left dirty screws on my tip trays instead of
dollars. The August night of the 1965 Watts Riots I stood on
top the roof of The Fort a tarpaper flat the size of 50 pool tables
where guys in the band partied during breaks. I watched the L.A.
sky glow orange neon fie-yarrr, black smoke cringe crow-slap
moustaches and pierce the sunset a van Gogh last earth dream.
As gunshots cracked and sirens screamed, I knew right then as I
read another indelible page of an unfolding starry, scary night, that
the book of my life would never be titled The Good Old Days.
But at least I'd have slo-mo shadow memories of dancing upon the
Whisky á Go-Go stage with Jim Morrison, and though a dirty
dive, The Fort was close to home and the parking space was free.

Concert Bal Tous Les Soirs

Even I, who'd only been in the two beer bars
I'd worked so far knew that The Fort
was a hellhole, knew that the Norwegian
wharf rats the size of cats
who watched me in the storage room
used as a dressing room were not Disney-esque
knew that the 7-foot-tall Samoan brothers,
the bouncers, two dragons wearing hornets' nest collars
who smacked sawed-off pool sticks across their palms
itchy for a fight, were not picturesque
and Carlita and the other go-go girls
with teen-age-made gang tattoos on their hands
and rumps who stole my tips were not black comedy
but from the nether world of mirthlessness.

The Fort, a beer bottle's throw away from
the L.A. Harbor was the kind of dive
you see in 1940s' B movies where bad guys
go to hire an assassin
the kind of place where even Genghis
and his horde would've sat
with their backs against the walls

and Crazy Ted, a Navy vet of two Big Wars
who'd received two Purple Hearts
who'd been knifed in dives from Pearl Harbor to Seoul
and crazy to boot, knew that The Fort
was the worst dive of them all because when
he walked in he rolled his eyes, pulled up
the collar of his Navy pea coat to hide his clenching jaws
and then as he sipped his beer, frowning
as if it were poisoned, he told me
Get the hell out of this place before it's too late
and while I was on the stage dancing the Temptation Walk
Crazy Ted snuck out, even though he always carried a gun.

And that night I quit
but not because of the screws that meant the obvious
some of the Bikers left on my tip trays

and not because of the drunken German sailor
who was out to get me
because he thought I stole his last dollar

and not because of the carload of the young Mexican guys
who waited for me down the road after work
and sang "La Bamba" and yelled "*PUTA!*"
out the windows of their rattletrap car
while they followed me to my freeway on-ramp

nor because of the gunshots I heard every night
coming from the railroad yard across from The Fort

nor because of the lumps on the side of the road
I saw every night and was sure were corpses

nor because of the evaporating dream
of getting rich quick as a go-go girl
working double shifts

but because

I missed my three kids.

Honeybee upon the Tundra

Shirley MacLaine's all over tv today, says she
believes in Reincarnation, in another life was
a princess, another time a scientist on Atlantis
and she hasn't had it too bad in this life either,
got to be a star on Broadway, play poker with
Sinatra, won Oscars, all her books've been best
sellers, plus she got to have Warren Beatty for a
brother. Why wasn't she ever a peasant maimed
by small pox and white and black plague and
bloodletting like the rest of us? I hate to imagine
what I was in Other Lives, a slave trader, maybe,
or a witch hunter or the one who lit the torch to
burn down the library at Alexandria because I
haven't had it so hot in this life, never got picked
cheerleader in high school 4 years in a row and
when a go-go girl my only sugar daddy was Crazy
Ted who tipped change from a dollar once a day
just before he passed out cold hugging his 20th
beer. My novel's never been published, I can't
even get a teaching job, the flywheel just conked
on my 1972 Dodge Dart, plus I'm sure that when
God hears what a Why Me-whiner I've been in
this life bemoaning my lack-of-status-&-gratis Fate,
for sure in my next life He'll smite my tongue as well,
make me be a beer can in the Garden, an umlaut in
Alsace-Lorraine or a honeybee upon the Tundra.

@ Naked Street & Reincarnation Way

If reincarnation is really real,
I do not wish to be reincarnated,
Tossed out into this cold world

Naked again. It's taken me all my
Life to find enough clothes to keep
My soul and skin warm and

I still don't know what to wear.

My Aunt Louise's Movie Star Game

My Aunt Louise was always ruining my childhood
with her Movie Star Game: "G.A.!" she'd suddenly say
on our way to the Colton Movie Theatre.

GENE AUTRY! I'd reply. "NO!" Louise'd say.
GLADYS APPLECORE! I'd say, trying again. "NO!
You know there's NO movie star named Gladys Applecore.
Be serious."

I give up, I'd say and she'd tell me the answer: "George Arliss."
WHO'S THAT?
"A silent movie star."
But you said we couldn't use silent movie stars.
"You can if they're not dead."

Then, 6 years older than me, Louise'd light up a Camel
she stole from her Daddy my step-grandpa to say, all grown-up:
"You lost. So it's still my turn: O.W."
OSCAR WILDE!

"NO. He's not a movie star. He's a director or something unimportant."
Oh, I give up.
"Orson Welles, Dummy," she'd say.

My turn at last: R.R.! "Rosalind Russell." NO. "Ronald Reagan." NO!
I'd say, feeling smart. "I give up," she'd say, and I'd rejoice:
ROY ROGERS!
"NO! NO! You can't use cowboys in my Movie Star Game.
I don't like cowboy movies."

But YOU used Gene Autry yesterday.
"I changed the rules today," she'd say.
But that's not fair, I'd always say, when she changed the rules.
"It's MY Movie Star Game and I can do what I want."
And then my Aunt Louise would blow smoke rings in my face,
fluff her dark hair, frown down at me, only 8 years old, and go on:

"A.L." ALAN LADD!

"Nope." ANGELA LANSBURY! "NO." Oh, I give up. I'd always say.
"Archibald Leach." WHO'S THAT? "Archibald Leach is Cary Grant's
real name." That's not fair. You keep changing stuff.

"MY game, MY stuff," she'd say, blow a smoke ring into the air.
My turn at last: C.C. "Claudette Colbert." NO. "Charles Coburn."
NO. "Oh, I give up." CHARLIE CHAPLIN! I'd exclaim. Then
another smoke ring while my Aunt Louise announced coldly: "Sorry.
NO silent screen movie stars unless they're DEAD."

But you just said you could use silent movie stars if they're NOT dead.
"I've changed the rules."
 But that's not FAIR.

"Sorry. It's MY game. I can do what I want."

WHY? When it's NOT FAIR! Then she'd always say:

"Because it's my PREROGATIVE."

And that's how I spent five miserable summers of my childhood
with my Grandma Viola in Colton, California, who never noticed
my young life being ruined by my Aunt Louise and her Movie Star Game

Yes, every little kid endures coming of age, rites of passages that teach
integrity, intelligence and perseverance that either

makes you or breaks you and for sure, no Catch-22 nor Gotcha Moment
when grown up ever came close to the ridiculous, nefarious confusion
I lived through playing my Aunt Louise's Movie Star Game that taught m

nothing

except how to pronounce Prerogative.

Viola Mae Linton Jobe, 1903–1983

My grandmother didn't know what graduate school was nor
what the masters of fine arts degree meant I was studying for;
she knew how to patchwork quilt, crochet, embroider lace, knit,
fry chicken golden Texas-style on a wood stove, bake biscuits,
butterscotch pies, make pants and dresses good as store bought;
my grandmother didn't understand that at university I taught
James Joyce and Virginia Woolf stream of consciousness;
she'd told of Noah's ark, David and Goliath, Job, Genesis,
Lot's wife, Jonah and the whale Bible tales in Sunday school;
my grandmother didn't know "y'all" was southern colloquialism;
she never read Toynbee or Bukowski nor knew of intentional fallacies;
she knew what moment after a March full moon to sow cotton seed,
knew to plant asparagus and bachelor buttons in shade, yellow roses
and rainbow zinnias in high noon sunshine, tomatoes near fence posts
to vine, sprawl wide to become fat, warm, red sugar; my grandmother
never learned to drive an automobile, set the vertical control on her
Magnavox television set, yet she knew how to foal a colt, stitch
dogs' ears chewed ragged by coyotes, load shotguns to shoot crows
away from her corn, when to pick peaches for canning, how much
salt to preserve beef for winter, what greens growing wild in fields
would make your stomach stop growling, which verdigris leaf
you should use for poultice wrap to stop pain and bleeding.
My grandmother never knew about tsunami, e-mail, blog, bling,
ba-da-bing; September 11 was her birthday, not a 2001 day
of infamy; she never saw a bar code, thong, heard about AIDS,
global warming, nor the Escherichia coli she'd die from one day
after surviving the Spanish influenza of 1917, German measles,
a Black Widow's bite, Texas drought, World Wars I & II, the Great
Depression and the death of her 48-year-old son; my grandmother
knew everything and nothing and after all the years I've spent learning
all and more of everything, I know I know small and less of nothing.

How You Taste the Apples

The winner of the Yolo County Fair's 1985
First Prize for Apple Pies showed me how
to keep my pie flute golden while it baked by
simply making an aluminum foil collar for
the pie pan like you might for the Tin Man's
whip-lashed neck and while she showed me
how to weave a lattice top for my cherry pie she
told me her apple pie won because of the
Gravensteins, those large, yellow, red-striped
apples she drove 40 miles to Sebastopol to buy
that are only ripe two weeks in July, the same time
her husband's parents came from Pittsburgh to
discuss her bad marriage getting worse and
while her husband and his parents drank Wild
Turkey bourbon in the living room, in her kitchen
she rolled out the pie dough made of lard and butter
(for a nutty flavor) and then she arranged inside the
pie crust the Gravenstein apple slices, apple half-
moons-halfmoons, a perfect swirl ad infinitum so that
when the apple slices baked down in their juice
the top crust would not go hard and fill with stale air.
Many highballs later, after her husband told his side
of the story, his parents came to the conclusion
that their son's obligations to his baby and wife
should not interfere with his personal happiness
or life and the last place her husband took her
before he went away was to the Yolo County Fair
and when she saw her first place blue ribbon
she covered her face to hide her tears, asked
him to leave her alone with her pie for awhile
so he carried their baby away to see the clown.
The main reason, though, she told me she won
was simply because those Gravenstein apples
are the perfect sweet-tartness for pies. You
don't have to add lemon or cinnamon or
sugar or spice. That way all you taste are
the apples.

Endless Summers

for my son, Danny Bryan Horgan

Those endless summers when my son
and his buddies were too young
to drive a car, I packed as many
boy-men sardines that would fit
into my VW Bug and drove them
to the Surf Theater in Huntington Beach
to see surf movies, The Endless Summer,
Saltwater Wine and when the surf was Up,
they strapped as many surfboards as the VW
surf racks would hold and I drove them
to the Huntington Beach Pier where they
learned the poetry of the sea, sailed
aquamarine and spindrift soup
while I lay on the sand
studying for grad school exams
trying to make something of myself
and tried not to wish I were one of them
and then all the way home I listened to
their teen-aged a-b-c's of "awesome,"
"boss" and "cool," the salt and
sun turning their hair golden till
autumn and time to go back to school

and now my son and his buddies,
the age I was back then, their sun-streaked
hair grown-up dark while they try to make
something of themselves, come surfing now
to get back into shape and my son
brings his children now to show them
the way of the waves, those endless summers
and those sonnets of sun, sea and salt
going on and on as endless as
always.

Innocent Bystander

Here
in this Long Beach city
by the sea
seldom do you ever see
lightning striking
crackling electric silver fire
wicked witch fingers
fatal neon across the sky
bandit blasts
from Beethoven thunder guns

and if you do see

it happens when
rain cloud winds
blow so hard
the ocean gets up
on its hind legs
and walks across the land.

Jack Kerouac Spodiodi, Charles Bukowski Wine

At age 15 I began to write stories on my father's
1942 Underwood, hunt and pecked up to 5 pages
long starring a perky protagonist resembling Debbie
Reynolds in love with heroes honest as Abe Lincoln.
Mailed them off to Saturday Evening Post, McCall's,
Colliers, Redbook, Ladies Home Journal, Seventeen
magazine and waited for the $1000 check to arrive,
enough for a year's rent, a trip to New York City to
sip Spodiodi with Jack Kerouac and by age 20 my
rejection slip pile stood high enough for a game of
Old Maid and when my life turned crazy, my days
ran away and I became a vegetarian holding on to
the wheel of a quivering meat conception, at age 35,
I learned to type up to 100 wpm on my IBM Selectric,
so I wrote 20-page stories and sold my first for $50,
barely enough for a week's rent and a bus ride to L.A.
to chug wine with Charles Bukowski. Age 41, at last
I sold a story to Paris Review for $275, only 2 week's
rent by then. And now I've got a computer, can blab-
blog a story or more a day, but publishers can barely
pay their own rent anymore so they send me instead
of money comp copies of their magazines containing
my stories I tuck away neatly into boxes beneath the
coffee table, my impecunious stories, my millions of
words, clever idioms, hyperbole and denouements
starring perky Debbie Reynolds and brave Honest Abe
Free Rent, mere cheeseburgers and beer—for silverfish.

My Poor Old High School

One of the oldest big old stucco buildings in Southern
California, my poor old Excelsior High School stands there
naked beige scarecrow on the corner of Alondra and Pioneer
empty and closed down now since 1981 for lack of enrollment
the Baby Boomers moving on with their teenagers to a newer
part of the county and I get tears in my eyes when I drive by
and see most of the windows boarded up, some of its old red
rooftop Spanish tiles missing like teeth gone from old age or
a prizefight. The math department has been leased to a day care
center, the cafeteria to a Vietnamese cultural center, the huge
auditorium condemned where upon its stage my junior year
Spring Swing I danced a Belafonte "Day-o, day-o" samba
with my girlfriend Jan giggling so much from stage fright
and sweet 16 giddiness I almost tripped on my feet. Later
the movie *Grease* was shot over there on the front lawn
John Travolta and Olivia Newton-John bopping, singing
"Who do you love?" love songs. But all was not jolly in the
supposed good old days at my old high school. Boys went away
to four wars during those decades and some didn't come back.
A Great Depression made kids quit high school to find work.
Gangs and drugs came. In that stadium over there our Varsity
team lost the Homecoming game. My senior year over there
on the way to the 4-H sheds past the English department I saw
boys wear jeans and their hair like James Dean and over there
across the street boys with cool cars parked where soon there'd
be a Cerritos College built. But now no more coolest cars in school
drive by my poor old high school closed down now. No more
mean-well teachers telling you you'll go far (you did/ didn't),
go to jail (you did/didn't). No more teenagers wizened with young
and cigarettes hang around the burger stand. No more toot-toot-tootsie
or boogie-woogie, be-bop-a-loo-la, surfin' safaris, sock hops,
California girls, Mustang Sallys, Mohair Sams swinging on a star
stayin' alive, la-la-la-la bamba cool cats rock around the clock.
My poor old high school is closed down now forever but still
stands there big fat old wise worn-out Buddha, Easter Island,

Stonehenge, patina'd Abraham Lincoln and seems as if it might answer from out the cracks of the mouth of its chain-locked front doors if we ask, ask just one more time that same question we asked when we were kids: How? How, dear gods and moon and stars: How did we all get so old?

In Sight of the Acropolis

As I grow older, as it usually goes for
those growing older, my mind-capacity for
remembering important, intellectual things
is diminishing, blowing away like smoke
in windstorm and I remember the romantic, in-
consequential things: the first Santa Claus I
ever saw, the color of my skirt and blouse my
first day as a shop girl at May Company, the names
of the songs Johnny Horgan, an Irish tenor, was to
sing when I married his brother but he couldn't
because of laryngitis. I remember the name of
the Greek woman who shared a maternity hospital
room with me who told me her brother drowned while
swimming in the Aegean Sea in sight of the Acropolis.
I remember the name of my first poem when I was
assigned to emulate Sylvia Plath in my first
poetry workshop. I remember the kind of wine
my Grandpa Jim drank on doctor's orders to settle
his sick stomach after driving my Grandma Ola
all the way from Colton, California to Sacramento
for my father's funeral. I remember where I hid
my pearl-handled letter opener, where I was
New Year's Eves of 1962, 1966, and 1989, poets
I owe letters to, and the Japanese word for the
Sumo wrestling move for frontal force-out I saw
last night on tv: my Aunt Lil with rouge on her
nose. Beige. "Love Me Tender" and "Only You."
Angelina. "Pagan Daddy." Blackberry. In my roll-top desk.
With Bill. Alone. San Francisco. Wilma Elizabeth
Mc Daniel, Annie Menebroker, and Jules Smith.
Yori-kiri.
Life's mysteries: finally solved.

More Secrets about Beans

Beans meant a lot to me
when a kid disliking meat
beans the favorite meal
my mother fixed but my
father who'd grown up in
Texas Dust Bowl poverty
where a pot of beans
was eking out a living
as well as Sunday supper
loved meat, T-bones, thick
roasts, pork chops. Meat
on his plate meaning not just
luxury, deliciousness and
plenitude but also, so he
thought, good health. So my
Texas mother's once-a-week pot of
pintos and cornbread because
she craved them was always a
meatless bone of contention
between them. Beans still
mean a lot to me, a big pot
of pintos my favorite soup to
cook, especially on a cold
winter day when I'm all alone
and its steam fogs up the
windows, encasing me, making me
feel special and wrapped-up
as if I were a good-news secret
and I love how the bean soup's bubbling
warmth actually speaks to me
and I understand
every word.

Trying on Their Souls for Size

There's not much left now of my
father's things, just a few of his
paintings and this little table
he made and painted white with
gold metallic trim to match my
mother's 1950s moderne décor
I keep in the kitchen now
to roll out pie dough on.

I wish my mother'd kept some of his
clothes so I could try on one of his
vests, put my foot into one of his
shoes to feel the print of his sole
pretend to be him, after all, I have
his bony knees, his need now to read
small print with a magnifying glass
and bite my fingernails into the quick.

It's so simple and strange and perfect
that no matter where they are
we are our parents, carry their
DNA rattling inside our ribcages
like pneumonia and ghosts

Look: there they are now, look
at them wait for us and watch us
try to perfect our grown-up gait
so's to be able to catch up.

What the Japanese Believe

The Japanese, so I read, believe that
where one dies, so stays the soul.

My father passed away on a rainy day
in his company car in his two-car garage
on Edison Avenue, in Sacramento, California

My mother and I found him slumped over the
steering wheel, the windshield wipers,
the last On-button he'd ever touch,
still going like crazy, trapped bats'
wings-bats' wings across his silent face.

Visiting Sacramento last week I stopped by
the old house to look for my father's soul
but the new owners had installed
wrought iron bars on the windows
chopped down the backyard sky-high maple tree
and that made me very sad how they'd
jailed my father's soul, didn't give it
a chance to climb to the top branch
of the maple tree to wave at the moon
and tell it to shine on us
and say Hello.

Born Not to Laugh at Tornadoes

It was the only time I ever saw my father
afraid, someplace in the middle of Texas
on our way in 1948 from California to
Dallas, a tornado out there, stick-still
on the edge of the world, black-circled
by a steel-cloudy sky, a tornado like an
exclamation mark in a small book so far
away but yet night behind my father's
left ear as he drove his black jackrabbit
1939 La Salle running for its life 100 miles
per hour, no storm cellars in those parts
not even a gas station, just dirt all around
and telephone poles toothpick horizon time
and that tornado curlicueing now like a
question mark and doing a little hula
next to my father's brow, my father chain-
smoking, grinding his teeth, my mother not
speaking, just twisting the radio knob
for tornado news or music or anything besides
static to drown out the wind outside blowing
Texas up our fenders. Were tornadoes coming at you
when they stood still or when they moved like
that? they asked each other but neither knew
they'd been little kids asleep in bed back then
in Texas when tornadoes hit towns nearby
and my father got that La Salle to do 125
on Route 66 for half an hour and finally
the tornado was behind us, only a comma now
and it began to pour-down rain, lightning
and thunder all around and in Denton the sun
came out and Hank Williams came on on the
radio and my father laughed and said,
"Christ, if that don't beat all."

Deep in the Heart of Texas

Other than the winter when I was born in
Paris, Texas, I've only been to Texas once
and on the way, right in the middle of Texas
near Denton or Sweetwater, someplace in
the middle of the night and nowhere where

there's not one tree or hill, one, just flat land
falling off the thousand corners of the Texas
earth, my father parked the car on the side of
the road and he, my mother and me got out
of the car to look at the stars, the sky a big

round black dome filled with so many sugar
crystalline stars that the sky dripped white as
vanilla cake icing and my father stood in
front of the car lights as if on a stage and sang
that song which should be Texas's state song

as loud as he could into the big, round-bright
night: "The stars at night are big and bright—"
and then he clapped his hand five times and
went on singing deep in the heart of Texas...

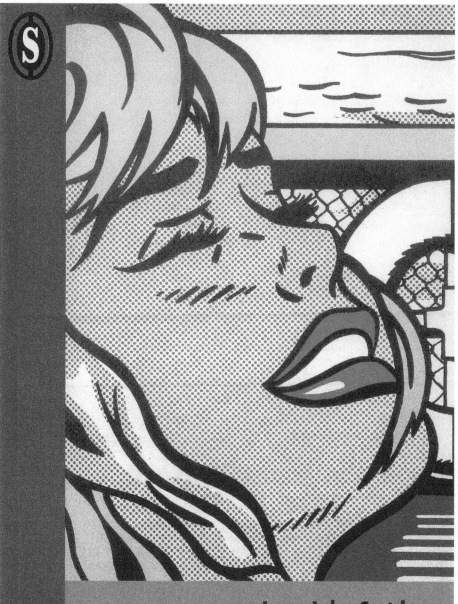

Joan Jobe Smith

The Pow Wow Café

The Pow Wow Café

To buy herself a new 1950s' moderne sofa
and wrought iron-framed repro of Picasso's
"Don Quixote" my father was too much
of a tightwad to buy her, my mother
got a job at the Pow Wow Café, a
truck stop on Highway 19 in Downey,
California where the waitresses wore
short, short red polka-dot skirts and
low-cut white peasant blouses that showed
half of my mother's baba au rum bosom.
"No!" bellowed my father while my mother
ironed her starched uniform into stiff
Mt. Everest peaks, not speaking to him
for trying to tell her what to do.
"No!" he bellowed as she drove away
to work her first night at the Pow Wow Café
and my father put up with this for
four nights, chain-smoking, biting his
fingernails, watching tv and come Friday night
he took my mother's short, short skirt
and low-cut peasant blouse and me to the
Pow Wow Café where he threw open the
manager's office door and threw my mother's
uniform onto the floor and bellowed
"My wife's not working in this
whorehouse anymore!" and then my father
sat down at the counter with all the truckers
ordered a chocolate sundae for me, coffee,
double cream for himself and told the
waitress when she brought them how nice
she looked this evening.

Pagan Daddy
After Sylvia Plath's "Daddy"

Neither of us thought to wonder, Daddy,
if weren't you afraid
after you said you knew for certain
when you died it would be IT.
Over. Finis. Snuffed out like
a candle and then you sliced with your finger
your throat and smiled a mischievous
grand finale, an elf playing tag
in the forest and never getting caught
but being consumed by the shadows
and the trees.
I disagreed with you, Daddy, and said how I knew
for certain of a spirit and an afterlife
and told you how science
had almost proved the existence of a soul
from the way the dead body diminishes
in body weight nearly evidencing
a release of Something
and you, the Baptist atheist, hardhead Texan
shook your head No and said they'd
never prove there was such a thing as a soul
in your lifetime
your committed finality a curiosity now
and how neither of us wondered if
weren't you afraid to die a noble secret
your savage determination not to be caught
an act of fugitive futility
as I'm left wondering in another darkness
bewildering the horror
of my own immortality.

MRI r i

Inside the cavernous bright white whale body of the
MRI, vibrating to the ear-busting, excruciating booms
bangs, sighs and groans of the sonosomethings to find
something wrong with me finally and the reason why,
I suddenly wonder why some people use the lower
case "i" and remember asking Bukowski why he did
and he said it was easier to type lower case nights he
wrote poetry on his manual typewriter drunk as a skunk
so I wrote poetry lower case for a while till I felt silly
and GROAN the MRI screams, barks BOOM! and the
universe is born! BOOM! a dinosaur falls into a smoky
abyss BOOM! and Sir Gawain's word severs the green
claws of a dragon and BOOM! your children are born.
Boom the sound of sea storm, world wars, a son saying
he doesn't hate you anymore, sigh, you never knew he
hated you, sigh, your back arches, chest heaves, your
breasts collapse as you clutch your Frida Kahlo T-shirt,
your MRI milagra, cotton long-sufferer Frida you wore
to protect you, be your bodyguard irony like Aretha
Franklin the day you played "Respect" on the North
Beach Condor Room jukebox in 1967 where you go-go
danced; r-e-s-p-e-c-t, you wanted but didn't get no; boom
burp MRI vomits you and you tell the scrupulous MRI
technician as he pulls you out of the white whale belly:
"My mother died in one of those."
"You're kidding," he says, not believing you.
"No, it's true, she really did." But to torture him the way
his MRI tortured you, you don't tell him doctors revived
her with CPR; just for a while, though, till she lapsed back
into her coma dying of that thing inside her brain you may
now have too so she didn't hear you yell at the doctors
DON'T HURT HER! nor did she know you ran the mile
in a minute down the hospital hall when you heard the
intercom cry CODE BLUE! how you ran right to the MRI
room though you didn't know where she was so she died
not knowing she wasn't alone, she died like we all do:

115

strange, sad, death shrouded in sneaky mystery. "You made it," says my poet husband in the car. "Frida will bring you good luck," he says, pats me, while my skull brims with booms, bangs, sighs of Bad News migraine memories, No, I say to him. No, and know I will never wear this soft cotton Frida Kahlo T-shirt ever, ever again.

Mother Two Moons: Look:

If I were you, you said to me in the beginning,
I'd carry you around on a feather pillow and
because I knew you would, Daughter who
always did what she ought to: I did what you
wanted the way you wanted: cooked your food
gently the way you liked it, and did, too, what you
did not ask: worried and wept while you, god
full, believing in prayer, promised me I would not
get sick like you. "This is not hereditary," you said,
and called me Strong Bones, the name you made up
just for me as we pretended to be Cherokee maidens
worried and scurrying in the tipi of your bedroom.
You never knew I named you Mother 2 Moons.
For your breasts, once white cake I mourned for
those three years as I watched them slowly disappear
upon and eclipsed by your accordion rib bones as
you grew sicker and smaller, bedfast as a flat satin
quilt tucked tough at the foot of the mattress grave.
Ten years after you died your DNA laughed at me
Gotcha in spite of your kindly god who promised you
I'd stay strong boned when old. It's a sad disease
as all diseases are but lonely now without you here to see.
But I show you anyway, say: Mother 2 Moons: Look:
Look how the blood of you flows through me and
burns my bones and brain crimson as I wonder why they
named the river near where we were born Red River.
Was it because of the rose pecans that fell into the
rage during storm and bogged the banks with fire?

Old Houses Creak and Moan All the Time

"…an uninhabitable planet/so far, far, far…"

Even though he'd never seen a dead body before
and didn't want to, my Poetry Man went with me
to the mortuary to see the dead body of my
second husband, Othello, who died at only 51
amazingly, peacefully in his sleep, in spite of my
ex-wife hexes

my Poetry Man going with me because he
was curious to see the man who tried
to kill me with his bare hands and we
looked at him lying there amongst the satin
and gladioli, looked at his huge, tan-brown
hands that once circled my young waist
then later my throat, his hand now
soft and graceful and harmless as sparrow wings
spread prayerful repose across his new blue shirt

we looked at his enormous head, his pursed
lips that once kissed me in long-ago
California moonglow, our Blueberry Hill
his lips now a smug smile as remorseless in death
as in life, a self-righteous satisfaction
no mortician could have posed postmortem
my dead Othello proving to us living that he
did it his way with fast horses, big cigars
young women and plenty of cream in his coffee and
red meat for dinner and as

my good husband, my last husband looked at
the dead body of my second husband
he understood me better, understood my
need for hyperbole I use to describe my life
that he knows now are really euphemism
to describe more gently the cold, hard facts
of the most extraordinary kind.

Dr. Cary Grant Becomes My Personal Brain Surgeon
after the 1950 movie "Crisis" and Philip Larkin's "Aubade"

Hollywood made a movie about my Meningioma,
Jose Ferrer playing Me, though I am not a tyrant
South American dictator nor do I wear a goatee,
combat boots or ever kidnapped Dr. Cary Grant to
remove my brain tumor. Dr. Cary Grant told Jose
surgery wouldn't work, Jose'd die anyway, his left
temporal lobe drowning in post-op hemorrhage, but
you know those rotten tyrants—they always get their
way. Fun watching that old movie and imagine Cary
Grant wearing doctor garb instead of tuxedo, Cary
scrubbing his hands to grab razor to shave my head,
then scalpel to trepan me, carve Cary luvs Joanie
on my scalp. Weird how on one of the worst days
I've had so far with this brain tumor I see that old
movie, learn more about me than I did from a brain
surgeon, neurologist, MRI technician and Google.
Weird how Jose Ferrer's seizure was just like mine;
Jose fell into bed like I do, tasered and teary-eyed.
But I don't carry a .45, can't point it at Cary Grant
and demand he heal me, remove this thing in my
head that rips my senses, smell, taste, touch, sight
and sound. I stare in time all the day, vowing not
to whine, waiting nothing more terrible, nothing
more true than withstanding the dread of this dying
to become dead, a movie that plays all day inside
my head as I lip sync the motion and emotions ad
nausea. If I owned a .45, instead I'd point it at
Cary Grant, make him take off his doctor garb and
wear a tuxedo and fly me in his wingéd limo to the
moonglow a go-go where we'd tango, waltz, cha-
cha-cha, and wa-Watusi into the zillion earth dawns,
pretend we'll never die—and forget sure extinction.

His Poems

for Fred Voss, 1989

I carry the poems he writes me in my
purse, everywhere, my new identification,
letters of recommendation, his words
and perceptions of me making me
more dark-eyed and shiny than
the eye shadow and lip gloss I carry.

His poems are what I hoped when I was
a girl to know when grown, that
first spring day I noticed how
the sun's rays turned to lace when
shining through leaves.

His poems were as faraway from me
then as that sun, and there would be
many months, years, and men to come,
without poems. but now, his poems
lay in my purse, waiting to be read:
my ink-written link, certificates
bone fide, to his creative soul
I now carry everywhere.

The Red River

A navigable river in south central United States, 1,018 miles
long, it rises in the high plains in east New Mexico, flows east
crossing the Texas Panhandle and then becomes a boundary
between Texas and Arkansas, turns south in southwest Arkan-
sas and crosses the border into Louisiana, flows southeast a-
cross Louisiana into the Mississippi River into the Gulf of
Mexico and I was born in Paris, Texas, 30some miles from
the Red River and first time I saw it in 1953 it was brown
muddy as old chocolate when we drove over it in my father's
new Ford Fairlane on Christmas Day to see my grandpa Old
Robert dying of TB in an Oklahoma hospital, my grandma Nora
weeping in the back seat beside me. I had to wait in the cold car
with the dog, little kids made old folks sick they said and on the
way back to Paris crossing over the Red River again my grandma
Nora told us about the big flood of 1914 when a big old 100-year-
old pecan tree like that big one over there fell over into the river.
Folks came for miles to save it, an Eiffel Tower, its roots Goliath
arms reaching for the sky. Hundreds of folks pulled and pushed
and tugged and heaved ropes tied to the tree trunk and branches
while the Red River raged wild and turned maroon and almost
drowned a lot of them. For days the folks camped out, stubborn
as only Texas and Oklahoma homesteaders can be and they saved
it just fine and come spring of 1915 the pecan tree rewarded the
folks with the biggest bumper crop ever known, horns of plenty
of plenty of pecans, three thousand pecan pies it must've made,
all the women doubling up pecans in each pie, four cups instead
of two, to float on top the brown sugar custard, not one pecan
orphan losing its way from that tree, not one pecan gone afloat,
uneaten Ishmael down below in that dirty old Gulf of Mexico.

The Nora and Dora Patchwork Quilt

My grandmother Nora and her twin sister Dora, age 83,
during their long hot Texas summer of 1973, made for me
a patchwork quilt. "Sorry, honey, Dora and me not faster,
but the needles slip out of our fingers the weather's
so humid," my Nora wrote me in California where we
had drought, dust turned my peach tree gray, heat
dried up all the fruit. But just in time for Christmas
the quilt arrived, a brilliant spread of cotton magic
I placed upon my daughter's bed, later covered three
granddaughters for sleepovers and when the quilt
frayed, I stored it away in plastic. Nora and Dora
never let me pay for all their fine, hard-hard work,
told me the scraps were free from their church folks
and last summer, long and hot like ones in Texas,
I remembered the quilt in my closet, so across my bed

I tossed its bright wide skycloud sunrises and sunsets,
memory mosaic patches of Texas Sunday-go-to-meeting or
Monday's go-to-school-or-work-or-coffee shop clothes,
stripes of blue, green, yellow, brown plaid from the
cowboy, farmer, truck driver, fix-it man or teacher's
shirt, aqua paisley from Old Annie's apron or Jennifer's
orange 8th grade skirt, red polka-dot sunbonnet, scarf,
green gingham kitchen curtain snips, black slashes off
back sleeves of Johnny Cash wannabes, tie-dye of the
town's only hippie—all of them picnicking now upon
my bed where my great-grandson, Gage, age 2, sits in the
midst of them, eating a cookie, touches for a crumb
next to one of the 100s of threads Nora or Dora sewed
so long ago time moment for some kin like him to find.

Getting the Hell out of Texas

California, here we GO! sang my father in 1948 as he
drove over the Golden Gate Bridge in his '39 black-shiny
LaSalle sedan, going back home to Texas. Homesick
after 5 years in San Francisco, he and my mother missed
the Red River, fireflies, Big Sky, cottonwood and pecan
trees and all their kin, Y'all Come-talking uncles, aunts,
my father's cousin D.J. An auto body man now, my father
would buy his own place in Dallas, save his money for a
cattle ranch. But that summer of '48 was the hottest streak
since the Dust Bowl days. The Red River nearly a creek,
cottonwoods made him wheeze, his cousins Joe and Bob were
now drunks, their kids made fun of me for using good grammar,
aunts and uncles called us heathen for not going to church on
Sunday. The heat blistered my father's pale Scottish skin,
chigger bites on my mother swelled pink and walnut-size,
100% humidity kept the cars my father painted from drying
for days and one 120-degree August day when Texas folks
joked "Hell is a lot hotter in Texas" and when heat rash broke
out on me from ears to knees, my father, while dabbing me
with Calamine said: We're getting the hell out of Texas. And we
did, my father driving that LaSalle 110 miles an hour all the
way on Route 66 back to California and ever since, when plenty
goes bad for me, me trapped between rocks and 100 hard places
and I don't know when to hold 'em or fold 'em, I always say
I'm getting the hell out of Texas and imagine my foot on the
gas petal of a big, black-shiny sedan flying full speed ahead,
making it from Dallas to El Paso's Rio Grande in a minute,
Pacific Ocean blue fog, Sequoia Edens of Everywhere shade
where things will never again go wrong—only one hour away.

Heart Garden

after becoming a great-grandmother at age 64

Remember when you were a young mother
and your children were born and one day
you pulled your child by the hand just in
time away from danger? Or said: Listen
to me! and suddenly it was your mother's
voice you'd heard and you laughed: I am
my mother! Perhaps this happened again
when you became a grandmother and then you
became her, too, except that there were two
of them and which were you? The Scottish
Viola Mae who fixed fried chicken and cream
gravy, made you a yellow sundress with
tiny pink daisies on the bodice? Were you
the tough German Nora who could shoot a
shotgun straight and brave as a cowpoke?
And now I am a great-grandmother and
wonder if there are four of me and if so,
I know names of only three: that Gypsy
fortuneteller, the dark-haired homesteader,
and the fair Scotswoman with melanoma
caused by Texas sun—those faraway women
my ancient vines veining bone and blood
heart garden, my bumper crop 40 fingers,
40 toes, four hips, tongues, lungs, eight eyes,
legs, arms, hands, feet, 128 teeth. If only I
could have all four here beside me to lend
eight hands when I need help from the tub, all
those ancient women's four hearts beating as I
stir soup and they whisper to me: Hello, You.

There

Now my mother's illness is so severe
she cannot walk by herself any more, she
must lean on a crutch I prop under her
right arm as she leans her left elbow
into the bow of my left arm and I hold
her tiny waist with both hands the way
my father used to when he
got the notion to kiss her and I sway
her hips to make a walking motion and
she breathes fast and asks:
Am I there?

During World War 2 when there
weren't enough buses and streetcars for all
the soldiers and sailors and the working women, too,
she had to walk every day 20 blocks from her
waitress job at the Payless Café in San Francisco to
my nursery school to fetch me and then she'd carry me
in the bow of her hip the 10 blocks
uphill home and now and then her hip would hurt so
and her feet would hurt so she'd have to
stop and put me down, take off her
high heels and breathe fast for a while.

Why didn't you make me walk too, I asked her
and she answered, Because
you would've gotten tired, too.

Me and My Mother's Morphine

The Governor of California and the DEA, my
mother's doctor says, keep close tabs on us
Californians' medical morphine use so I must
drive five miles once a week to fetch in person
The Triplicate, a beige, crisp piece of
paper, as dear as a cashier's check, to
take five miles to the other side of town to
the only pharmacy that carries my mother's
liquid morphine. On the way, I stop at
Trader Joe's for mine, the California kind:
green syringes of cabernet sauvignon, Eye
of the Swan, pinot noir, chardonnay, I
later sip to blur Life while I spoon feed my
bedridden mother her supper.

"Now I know why you drink wine," she says,
a teetotaler, a good Christian woman who's
never approved of my wine-drinking. "Being
doped up brings you closer to God," she
says, seeing Sistine things now upon
her ceiling, fidgeting and licking her
dry lips, the one-half cubic centimeter of
morphine, the same color blue as Windex,
I give her mornings and bedtime in apple
juice more potent to her 60 pounds than
a $200 hit of heroin to a prickled L.A. junkie.

Sad now and ashamed of her addiction as much
as her illness, sometimes she weeps as she
sucks through a straw the last drop of
morphine from the cup, and sometimes I
imagine the Governor of California and his DEA
boys breaking down my mother's bedroom door—
Conquistadores roaring "Eureka!"—coming to prick
their spears at mother and daughter us: a couple
pagans all right, red-eyed and doped up, naked
with sin and death.

On the Way to Heaven

She nearly died the year before she
really died. I saved her, gave her
mouth-to-mouth, pounded her chest
like they do in the movies—bruising her—
until she came to and like in the movies
she smiled, looked around and asked
"Where am I?" and when I told her and
that I'd brought her back to life she said
"Oh, no, you ruined everything, I was
on my way to heaven, heard angels singing.
I was all dressed in white and had no more pain."
She wept all morning.

In the afternoon she called me into her
bedroom and sternly told me that if that
ever happened again, not to save her.
I told her I couldn't help trying to save her
that something stronger than me inside me
made me do it, a reflex perhaps from the womb
like when she'd yank my hand in time to
save me from being run over by a car.
She screamed at me all afternoon
from her bedroom how I'd ruined it for her
and would ruin it again and I screamed back
how sick I was of all this: the bedpans, the
morphine, my keeping her alive for her to
wish she'd die. Such ingratitude!
We both wept till dinnertime.

While I fed her dessert of vanilla ice cream
she cleared her throat, letting me know
more was to come but she apologized
instead, thanked me for saving her life.
"I know now how much you really must love me,"
she said, "to save this old bag of worthless bones."
And then she laughed for the first time in a long

long time. I wanted to hug her but I couldn't
for her pain. I'd never hug her, I knew,
ever again but it felt good to both of us
when I cooled her bruises with a little
witch-hazel-soaked cotton swab.

Margie Jay

As she lay dying upon, as she named it, her Mattress
Grave, my mother confessed to me Things From Her
Past, one of her most shameful in 1942 when she was
asked to go on the road, be Girl Singer with a swing
band heading for Albuquerque, Santa Fe, Phoenix, LA,
Hollywood, San Fran and then Reno. She'd've changed
her name to Margie Jay, worn tight-fitting ball gowns,
shiny Red Rose lipstick, pink rouge cheeks, gardenias
moonlighting her long chocolate hair and sung love songs
Stardust, Night and Day you are the one, Body and Soul
deep in the heart of me in her sweet soprano voice while
sweethearts danced, saying Goodbye in World War Two
to tunes with cool-jive saxophone, clear-hearted trumpets
and an occasional wild Gene Krupa backup drum solo.
My mother, as Margie Jay, might've sung on the radio,
cut a record, later maybe been on tv like Dinah Shore,
wore a mink stole instead of an apron while she sang
solo each night in her kitchen while she fixed my father's
Texas-style supper and then washed dishes, me drying.
And while I fed my mother in 1986 her cream soups or
ice cream while she spoke of what might have been, she'd
smile, imagining faraway things that almost were and I'd
ask: "Why didn't you go on the road and be Margie Jay?"
And, being my mother, she said: "Because I couldn't take
you with me. The boys in the band didn't want a little baby
on the road and I'd've missed you too much." And how
I wanted to kiss her or hug her for loving me so much but
we were mother and daughter from another generation when
old-fashioned reprimands Be Good, Do Right were mistaken
as expressions of Love. So I kept her safe and clean, fed her
well, knowing our ineffable love translated clearly, though
unspoken as foxtrot music decades old, sweetly unforgettable.

If she were here right now I'd kiss her hair

She hated her hair. Chopped it short Leslie Caron
or Alcatraz inmate. Thinned it, yanked it,
slicked it flat with white crème de blanc.
Sometimes I'd hear her weep as she winced into
the mirror and combed her beautiful thick, black
curly hair and moaned, Oh, this old ugly hair of mine!

Her father's mother, my great-grandmother, had been
a Gypsy fortuneteller and my mother was so ashamed
and I never understood Why when I wanted hair
like hers, look like her instead of me, dish-watery
blonde scrawny hair she curled into good ship
lollipop Shirley Temple girl while she pinned
gardenias into her hair like Billie Holliday, poofed
her hair swirly atop her head like Maureen O'Hara hair

and one night, her hair pigtailed, when she kissed me
goodnight, leaned over me, came close, each
pigtail brushed against each of my cheeks,
each warm dark chocolate-colored plait
hello-caress, each curly tip a kiss, two kisses
at the same time as the kiss from her lips
to make me a sweet, sweet goodnight, sleeping tight.

Why Isn't There a Tenth Muse Named Margie?

Forgive me Erato, Euterpe, Terpsichore, Calliope,
Clio, Thalia, Urania, Polyhymnia, Melpomene,
when I don't listen to you. You know I love you,
all of you, but today my mother Margie talks to me.

I tried not to listen to her today while I thanked you all
for what you've meant to me since I was a child and
heard your whispering knowledge of music, poetry,
tragedy, history, dance, and the stars but you're all

so Grecian, ancient, while Margie talks to me of Texas,
still sings to me Cole Porter and Artie Shaw, teaches me
boogie-woogie and the world too much with us as she
explains god, the stars, my sun sign of Aquarius, Leo Moon.

Margie sings, weeps, prays, dances and soars like a comet
in the dark universe of my blood, just as your mothers do
in yours, dear Nine Muses. Who were your mothers, your Eves,
sweet beauties? I hear them crackle starburst as they breathe

sugar and fire around me and you, to tell me they know well
my Margie.

11 a.m. Just like Edward Hopper's Redhead

I lean toward my pied à terre window where I live, to gaze
out at the downtown Long Beach, California cityscape.
Except I'm not a real redhead, my real hair's really grey,
and I'm not naked.

I see the green hula-dancing palms, the Jupiter-sized
camellia tree fat with enough pink blossoms to confetti surprise
a yellow brick road to Hawaii.
I see the two-story apartment buildings next door and other side
of the alley, and telephone poles pointing the way to the reach-for-the-sky
Villa Riviera, the long-ago swanky hotel now a condo with ye olde
verdi-gris copper rooftop when lit up at night glows emerald cabochon
while its spy-eyed grim-grey gargoyles on the eaves glower and squat
and curse dread and dare demons to impale upon the spiked turrets.

At age two during World War 2
I could see all that out my bedroom window
when we lived on the Old Pike (before the city tore it down to make
land fill and a marina), the happy rattletrap roller coaster roars only a
block away from where I played with my dolls near boogie-woogie
hamburgers, jitterbug sailors paying a dime for a shoeshine, each
awaiting Long Beach cityscape sundown black-out
so's the Japanese bombers wouldn't see us down here near
the Pacific Ocean sand, everyone in the world wondering: What's next?

and now, here in 2015,
3 weeks after my 75th birthday, at 11:19 a.m., I remember
it's time to take out the trash to the alley dumpster, leave out food
and recyclables for the homeless, who, noontimes wander there,
worry, wondering, "What's next?" the way I do, too, inside here
with my dyed red hair as I look out my cityscape window,
waiting, wondering, "What's next?" just like
Edward Hopper's 11 a.m. naked lady does, too (doesn't she?), as she
leans, sighs, at whatever in her 1926 cityscape makes her remember and see.
Except I'm not naked.
Or am I?

Another Mauve and Pink Rosebud Print Sofa Dumped in the Alley

"Anger is a righteous emotion."
—Martin Luther King, Jr.

Yet another eviction from that green stucco low-rent
apartment building across the alley as that mean landlord
shoves into the dirty dumpster a sweet mauve and pink
rosebud sofa. Such a pretty sofa: plump, comfy and ruffly,
made in the good old 1990s romantic days of Princess Diana
ruffly mauve and pink rosebud home décor and bridesmaids
frocks when homelessness was an aberration soon to be
corrected—I was sure of it—by those who care. Not become
the norm of today when only millionaires and careerists
can pay the exorbitant rent here in our fair city, and when
mean landlord slashes the mauve and pink rosebud sofa
cushions, making sure no one can ever re-use for his own

because he hates the homeless, says they should just get jobs, I
feel sick. Impaired with hyper-empathy these dysphoric days this
world is too much with us, I try to take T.S. Eliot's advice
to care and not to care, try to look away as I dump my trash
of old poems and empties, but instead suspect Eliot was a liar
or bipolar, because my poet pals Bukowski and A.D. Winans
would write an objectively-correlatived diatribe; Neruda, though,
transcend with "I am a poet, not a politician." But dear poet Wilma
Elizabeth McDaniel reminds me that "I am an old woman and
must tell the truth." But when the mean landlord comes to dump
a big load of his evictee's mauve and pink dishes and clothes

I don't tell the truth; I lament: "Sure was a pretty sofa." Nor do
I transcend when mean landlord does not care as he grunts and
stinks of rancor and cigars as the harpies who care too much in
my blood groan to jump out my veins to rip off his head. And as
the Maenads in my migrained medulla, dire and drunk with not
caring screech to kick that mean, cheap landlord's ass to the
moon, I am instead, fair lady Princess Diana, and say: "Have a
nice day," croaking it, choking on the erosion of it to stifle my
twisted Tourette's syndrome sister, psycho-murderess Lady Macbeth,
and hide, Harridan Hypocrite, a bag of food I leave each day for the
homeless to find behind the telephone pole where he can't see.

133

Tinker Bell Sin Taxi

"...warm crayon/I wondered what color you'd be..."

Christmas Day, stirring turkey gravy on the stove, I
listen to my daughter explain to me what the doctor
explained to her about why she can't think or talk
right since her many strokes after the first one 4 years ago.
You see, she says, waving her fingers in circles around
her head, the nerve sin taxis [synapses, I amend] got to
find their way around that part of my brain that died
after my first stroke, they got to search around through
the stuff and find a way out my cord axe [cortex] all the
way up to the barn seniors [brain centers] to tell my
drain [brain] to tramp slip [translate] so it can tell my
tongue what to say right and while my daughter's
speech falters, her brain pondering the way she did
when she was age 8, I can't help blaming myself
for all this. I shouldn't've let her eat so many cookies
when she was a baby, given her more bananas, maybe,
for the potassium. Maybe vitamins, too. If only I'd
painted her room pink, she'd've stayed in the pink.
Taken her to church more so God could've blessed her.
Hired an Einstein to tutor her in parabola and moon
glow. Tinker Bell to teach her to fly, Mickey Mouse
to make her laugh more, a Little Mermaid to teach her
to swim so she wouldn't sink. If only her ex hadn't taken
to cocaine, caused her life to change, become so hard
on welfare, food stamps. She could've been a fashion
model with her slender legs, beautiful face and she
might've skied Jackson Hole this Christmas like so
many women her age do, marry an Ashton Kutcher
as a movie star her age did. If only—I berate myself
forlornly, stirring turkey gravy for Christmas dinner—
and then I notice how the circles she fingers over and
over her head have become to look like halos and then
I realize she's becoming an angel before my very eyes.

Microwave Love Songs

Microwave, 1984. No room in the kitchen for that new
fangled invention, ugly rectangular thug, noisy arriviste
invading space of a bread box and my heirloom cookie
jar. I hated its blasted electrical thrum rot-zaps, the cause
perhaps of melanoma, tsunamis and my tennis elbow.
I missed wooden spoons stirring simmer stuff over low
flame till done, didn't trust one minute this thing from
outer space though for three decades I rearranged molecules
of 1 million suppers and one great-grandson's applesauce.
Cole Porter (not his real name, of course) gave me that
microwave on my 44th birthday. Cole Porter I now call him
for the tapes he gave me of Frank Sinatra's Night and Day
you are the one and deep in the heart of me I got you under
my skin I'd sing along in my green car on my way to his
Silver Lake place too tiny for a microwave so we ate to-go
Chinatown dim sum, Olvera Street tamales and tacos until
I wed a poet and he married a blonde and all the world's
surreal-mad machines zapped on till last week when my
old microwave caught fire. Only Krakatoa crackled louder
as firefighters rushed to the scene, lugged the charred thing
to the alley dumpster and told me: "Old things are dangerous."
Meaning me? Age 44 no more? Two fingers were burned
in the fire, ache whenever I yank open the shiny door of this
new microwave and turn the knob to watch the suppers spin,
chocolate melt, vegetable lasagna steam as I listen to the
molecules rearranging, thrumming, zapping proteins and
worrying me just like the old microwave did for 24 years.
Except this time I hear no love songs as I continue to wait
for the green so I can finally become a Safety Queen.

Joltin' Joe

I've begun to drink from The Joe
DiMaggio Cup I've kept put away for
years, a black, rather pretty thing
with a wing-like handle Joe DiMaggio
drank cappuccino from I served him
one night when I worked as a cocktail
waitress in a swanky hotel and when
Joe DiMaggio didn't want a second one
I snuck the cup into my purse.
Joe DiMaggio's lip prints were washed away
years ago but I like to imagine them
still there handsome-thick, dark Italian
barely middle-aged next to mine as I
sip from The Cup and wonder: if only
I hadn't asked him something personal
about Marilyn Monroe, maybe he might've
flirted with my fishnet stockings
and asked me my name.

Sending Sinatra Back to Heaven

Dreamed again last night I was a go-go girl
again, still thin enough to wear a bikini, toes
still tough enough to go-go dance in high heels,
my ancient bosom still push-up-able, am able
to carry two pitchers of beer in each fist even
though I haven't been able to open a pickle jar
since 1998 but just like all those other recurring
Ancient Go-Go Girl dreams, I'm terrified knowing
how the other go-go girls and the guys in the band
and my mean Simon Legree boss Spike will all
laugh at me when they find out the Truth: that I
snuck into this go-go bar I worked in so long ago.
They'll think me a pervy old broad spying on them
in their rock-out house of cool and groovy. And
making things worse last night, Frank Sinatra
wanted to date me, come fly with him, have one
for the road after I got off work and I didn't want to,
didn't know what to do: Tell him: Hey, Frank, this
is just a dream? In real life I'm a married woman?
I'm really 700-years-old and besides, Frank, you're
DEAD! But I can't tell Frank Sinatra that; it'd make
him mad; can't tell him either we have nothing in
common: Frank's a Sagittarius and bossy. Frank'd
make me wash his socks and bake lasagnas every
day and I'm a lazy but law-abiding Aquarian and
I'd call the cops when he hung with the Mafia and
then I'd have to go on the lam, hide out in a dark
room to write a poem about him like I'm doing
right now in Real Life after I woke up an hour ago,
sending Frank Sinatra back to heaven where Frank
belongs for singing all those beautiful love songs.
And then, having nothing else to do, I baked my
husband a great big vegetable lasagna and washed
his socks. I'm not so lazy after all and I'd really had
a really, really hard day's night—being young again.

Old Go-Go Girls Never Die

"Old soldiers never die, they just fade away."
—General Douglas MacArthur

—they just fray away, laughed the guys. Get it?
they'd ask, pointing to the beer-stained fraying-
away fringe on our bikinis. The guys, Shaden-
Freudians, liked the idea that us young girls'd
get old, fat and gray someday—hopefully soon so
they could say No to us like we did to them and as
us go-go girls watched the times a'changin', the
go-go thing go topless, bottomless, porn movie
theaters (the future horror of female mud wrestlers,
nude pole- and lap-dancers surpassing even our
cynical imaginations), us girls moved on, covered
up our bellybuttons, threw away our frayed bikinis,
crammed our bods into business suits to stagger as
shell-shocked as Vietnam vets into alarm-clocked
mornings, lit-bright coffee offices with screaming
telephones, mind-clattering typewriters instead of
jukeboxes. Old go-go girls good at math became
real estate brokers, know-it-all girls went back to
college for teaching creds or PhD's. Judy G who'd
dated a Righteous Brother managed his rock 'n' roll
nightclub. Nila, President of Dick Dale's Fan Club
became his Girl Friday. Mitzi's husband got rich on
Wall Street and they moved to a posh gated community
with a golf course. Brandi Blue and Linda Lee learned
computers and moved to Silicon Valley. But by the 21st
century they'd all disappeared. Where did all those old
go-go girls go? I wanted to know. Repeat to them the old
go-go girl joke all those guys liked best: How many
go-go girls does it take to screw in a light bulb? None.
Because go-go girls screw in waterbeds. Get it? I'd
ask all the old go-go girls and they'd get it all right
and groan ho-ho while they sip the imaginary tea I
make them right now, laced with cognac or tequila,
crystal meth or absinthe or Botox or Ben & Jerry's
Cherry Garcia, whatever nepenthe it takes these craziest days
of all those go-going days to keep girls from fraying away.

Virginia Woolf and Me Minding the Generation Gap

Dustin the teen boy next door asks me about my
red Virginia Woolf T-shirt I wear on my birthday:
"Who's that?" and I tell him and that I was born on
her birthday along with Robert Burns and Somerset
Maugham and Dustin winces, looks confused and
a bit nauseous. A British writer, I try to clarify and
he frowns, bobbles his shaven head atop his baggy
rock concert logo'd T-shirt, his scrawny knees
wriggling out of his baggy britches. Dustin looks
like every stay-at-home white boy from L.A. to
New York City who surfs the internet and plays
with his smartphone all day and smokes pot all
night so it would make no sense to him if I told
him I'd read *Mrs. Dalloway* in grad school years
before his birth, had tried to write like Virginia
Woolf, used a lot of semi-colons and streams of
consciousness so I say: Virginia Woolf wrote songs
for the Beatles, played tambourine for Sid Vicious,
was Posh Spice's great-grandmother and that makes
Dustin smile, say "Hey, yeah, way cool, I thought
she looked familiar." Then he answers his cell, struts
cool dude down the street to go to the corner 99-cent
store to buy cheapo cigarettes and I go to the super-
market for milk and think what fun it is not to tell
the truth, feel as giddy from this flippant fabrication,
my flummery of balloon juice as I'd be from chugging
a magnum of Dom Perignon champagne so I pat
Virginia Woolf on her tousled upswept Victorian
hairdo printed on my red T-shirt and thank her for
Being There for me, but Virginia Woolf only hmmphs,
not speaking to me, too good for me, just like always.

Cauliflower

At the Farmers Market yesterday
amongst the leaves and grasses
of basil, cilantro, asparagus,
avocados, tomatoes, onions
red, yellow, and white, across
from the Mexican woman singing
fiesta and not far from the
saxophonist crooning Bird, I saw
the most beautiful cauliflower
I'd even seen: huge, the size of
a dinner plate, the face of a
Rabbit moon, taking two hands
to hold it, big as 30 handfuls of
thirsty water. But we don't
care much for the taste of
cauliflower so I didn't buy it,
a bargain for two dollars and
I walked on to buy garlic and eggs
but later, I still thought about
that cauliflower: the bright dunes
and lacy crevices of it, how beautiful
it would look in a bowl like a bouquet,
a crystal ball, uneaten, while it told our future
read our maps to the gold of our souls
but when I went back to buy it
the cauliflower was gone
off to another's home to be steamed,
eaten, and add 20 years to their lives.
And I suppose it was good that I
did not buy that cauliflower.
I am too ordinary for such power.

Hot Tamales

Marion, *mi comadre*, has spent three whole days
preparing the ingredients for her Christmas tamales
20 pounds of beef she simmered on the stove until
the meat fell from the bones, then shredded by hand
into the chile sauce Marion made from New Mexico
deep red chiles and then made the *masa* with garlic
and lard Marion kneaded at least an hour until a ball of
the yellow-white corn mush floated in a cup of water
the sign at last the *masa* will not be flat and stick to
the corn husks when cooled but be tender and plump
the corn husk wrappings coming off smooth as silk
when you unwrap the perfect miraculous hot tamale
and this Christmas Marion asks me to be part of this
Mexican tradition, join her woman assembly line with
Marion and her daughters and nieces, each of us with
aprons and a pile of washed and dried golden corn husks
upon which we spoon and spread (on the *smooth* side)
the amber *masa* and then dollop chili meat in the middle
and then roll and wrap and tie the tamale with a ribbon
of torn corn husk one by one, one by one, one by one
while we women talk of men, babies, the glory of God,
Jesus the reason for the season, away in the manger on a
silent night and jolly old St. Nick, sleigh bells, halls of holly,
fa la la and white Christmas, blue Christmas, green bright
O Christmas tree, O Christmas tree and angels and Rudolph
and red noses and hey, baby, merry Christmas. Christmas,
we see, was when love was born, a halting time of hate as
we each speak and sing until one by one we've made 100s
of tamales for Marion to carry in the biggest pot I've ever
seen to steam for hours on the stove as the tamales slowly
slowly cook and cook while we women wait there in this
glorious, delicious state in this steamy kitchen universe
aromatic with corn, garlic, red chiles, *feliz navidad* and
hot tamales.

Uncle Ray on New Year's Day Long Distance from Hot Springs, Arkansas, Calls to Say

He's just had his 3rd pacemaker installed. They
(the HMOs) make you wait now till the old ones
break down so he couldn't move for 6 whole days;
couldn't take no anesthesia while they did the new
one, he's almost 85, too old, so they did a local but
he's okay and I say, Oh, goodness (hating HMOs).
But he can take it, I know: Uncle Ray's had a metal
plate in his head since age 18 when he escaped twice
in World War 2 from 2 German POW camps and he
goes on to say my cousin Charles Douglas Smith
down in Austin got hit and got run down by a drunk
woman driver on his motorcycle (Uncle Ray's two-
step Texas syntax, not mine) and after two surgeries
Doug's okay and Uncle Ray says he read that poem
of mine I sent him about the Red River. Did I know
they once lived right by it in Texas and Yes, I say
and one time his Daddy the cowboy, my granddaddy,
herded cattle across the Red River when it was a mile
wide and I imagine a mile-wide Red River, raging
bittersweet chocolate and wonder: How's it possible
to cross a mile-wide river without a bridge? Wonder
how's it possible to escape twice from 2 POW camps
with shrapnel in your head? Stay alive through open
heart surgery without anesthesia? Motorcycle miracle,
Pacemaker catastrophe and Uncle Ray says did you
hear about all them blackbirds that dropped dead out
of the sky yesterday here in Arkansas? Yes, I say and
he says how he and my Aunt Ernestine will be married
65 years come June and they don't send Christmas cards
no more because Ernie can't hold a pen to write no more
and Uncle Ray don't know how to spell—ha-ha-ha—he
laughs—because he only went to 3rd grade. But you're a
hero, escaped twice when you were only 18 from German
POW camps during World War 2, shrapnel in your head,
I say, and Uncle Ray laughs again and says, Aw, honey,
if it'd happened to you, you'd'a done the same thing.

The French're Much Different from Me and You

Uncle Ray on Christmas Day did not call
from Hot Springs, Arkansas, the way he
has for the past ten years to say: Howdy
Niece, How're y'all? so I could say, Uncle
Ray, I went to Paris last summer! *France*,
Uncle Ray, not Paris, Texas, where I was
born in 1940 and Uncle Ray in 1923. Paris,
France, where he, a G.I. Joe in 1945 marched
down the Champs-Elysees with his troops on
his way to the Arc de Triomphe to receive a
Croix de guerre from General Charles de Gaulle
for bravery for escaping twice from Nazi POW
camps and saving his men from machine guns.
Wanted to tell Uncle Ray I'd thought of him as
I strolled that same path, 2012, perhaps my
red sandals stepping in the same spot as Uncle
Ray's brown, worn-down 1945 Army boots.
I was brave, too, dodging traffic, motorcycles,
bicycles, taxis, limos, Rolls-Royces, to stand
in the middle of the Champs-Elysses to take
a photo of the Arc de Triomphe to send him.
Uncle Ray would've laughed at that and for
sure told me again how General de Gaulle
after he pinned the Croix de guerre on my
Uncle Ray's chest, kissed both of his cheeks.
"General de Gaulle didn't mean nothing by it,
honey," Uncle Ray might've said again. "Men
kissing men like that's just the way the French do.
The French're much different from me and you."

I Got YOU, Babe

My good Poet Husband doesn't like it when I write a poem
about us using his nom de plumes Frank and Jane he uses
when he writes domestic psychodramas about us.
Why can't I use Frank and Jane, too? I ask him.
"Frank and Jane're MY names!" he growls.
Why are you so possessive of Frank and Jane?
"You're plagiarizing me!"
Imitation is the best form of flattery, I say. Why aren't
you flattered that I like the names Frank and Jane?
Are you being competitive with me? Your Poet Wife?
"Be poetic, then. Make up your own names."
How about Sonny and Cher? I sneer.
"Don't be ridiculous," Poet Husband snaps back.
How about Frida and Diego?
"I'm not FAT!"
How about Camilla and Charles? Charles is bald like you.
"We're working-class Proletarians!"
How about Charles Bukowski's Hank and Wanda?
"We're not Barflies."
Gable and Lombard? Bogie and Bacall?
He likes those names but says they don't sound literary.
Scarlett and Rhett? "Cliché." Okay. How about Bride of
Frankenstein and the Monster? He frowns, says,
"We're not monsters!"
Othello and Desdemona? Because your obstinance is killing me!
He glowers, says "That's not nice."
Brad and Angelina? Will & Kate?
But Poet Husband doesn't know who they are and by then I've
forgotten my poem I was going to write about us so I
leave him alone to re-read Beowulf and I go into the bedroom
to watch my favorite tv chef prepare prosciutto-wrapped
tapenade-topped ahi and remember that Ernest Hemingway
once wrote that bickering is a form of entertainment yet
I don't feel entertained a bit. I want to throw an ashtray at him
like Lana Turner does at John Garfield in that old movie
The Postman Always Rings Twice except we don't smoke.

Aboard the Pequod

All week my Poet Husband's been reading
for the 5th time *Moby Dick*.
I watched him set sail from Nantucket
in his Toyota while I grocery shopped, he
sharpened his harpoon while I got a pedicure, he
drank grog while he listened to Charlie Parker and
Miles Davis and The Doors, he battened the hatches
in bed while I watched a Bette Davis movie on tv, he
yelled thar she blows in the bathtub while I
washed breakfast dishes and now and then he'd
put away his book and sit beside me and give me a kiss
In Port, I'd say, to visit his Lady Faire and then he'd
go back to sea, an atlas beside him so's to chart
the Pequod's course through the Indian Ocean
across the equator down to Java, the Cape of Good Hope
and when he was finished reading Melville, he
rented the movie video and was furious at
Ray Bradbury's screenplaying-around making
Queequeg a white man, making Moby Dick into a King Kong, a
mere bete blanche of Hollywoodian special effects and he
was so furious he turned off the movie and to cheer him
lure him from his unhappiness with the modern world
I fixed him a seaman's supper worthy of his
book-bound week at sea: I fried him some cod,
stewed a pot of clam chowder, baked some
hardtack and I watched him eat as he continued to
stare into space, still out to sea
remembering Melville's leviathan words and I waited,
served him more chowder, poured more grog, waited
for the Real Ishmael to paddle past all that Ahab madness
and come back to shore to me.

Mopping Floors Naked

Never in a gadzillion years
would Charlie Parker ever
have imagined that someday
while his "April in Paris" played
his Bird life comin' out his horn, that a
Poet Man would listen to his LP
turned up full blast while
mopping floors
naked
(well, almost naked as he wears
his baggy boxers with hearts on them).
And I'm feeling Kakfaesque
and Oracular
for having thought
of this wise, wild absurdity
as I watch this Theatre of the Absurd
as Poet Man huffs and puffs
mopping the floors
naked until he says,
rinsing out the dirty mop:

"Why not?"

What I Learned from the Movies

When I hear shocking news, I will faint.
When my fiancé leaves me holding a candlestick on the haunted house staircase to go for help 20 miles away, the vampire will bite my neck. When my fiancé and the bad guy begin to fight over the nitroglycerin/ uranium or something that will destroy every living thing on earth if spilled, I will hit on the head with a Ming vase, baseball bat or Maltese falcon—my fiancé. When the handsome singing cowboy who saved my life and my father's ranch from the dastard banker or Apaches kisses me and rides off into the horizon on his white horse, I will smile and disappear. When I am in the family way and ride a horse or walk down stairs, I will fall and lose the child I am carrying, When my child coughs or sneezes, he/she will die. When my child dies, my husband will blame me and I will take to streetwalking and drinking whisky with stevedores along the wharf, lose my looks and will to live and throw myself beneath the wheels of a locomotive or a black La Salle sedan. When a telegram arrives, it will always tell me that my fiancé has died in the war. When the moon is full, a man will either kiss me or kill me. When I wear marabou and contemplate suicide while gazing at the Manhattan skyline, Fred Astaire will ask me to dance. When Elvis tries to kiss me on the balcony, a gang of girls will ask him to sing while they push me over the railing into a swimming pool. When Marilyn Monroe is near, I will suddenly bear a striking resemblance to a bean and egg burrito. When I am 40 like Blanche Dubois, yet still have smooth crème fraiche skin, I will place paper lanterns over light bulbs of desire to hide my aging face to spare young men from shrinking from the hideousness of my old woman-ness and when I am 50 like Norma Desmond, even though I still have skin as smooth as cream cheese, I will beg for a close-up so's to terrify every man on earth with my antiquity and when I am 70 or more and must scrub floors to earn a living, I will work on my hands and knees with rags and buckets while the men use mops and smoke cigars. And: when I cry Oh! and they call for a doctor and he tells them to boil water, I will die.

Dear God

Thank you, God, for not turning me into a giraffe
when I was 5 and wanted to be tall. Thank you
for never bringing me a baby sister or brother;
he/she surely would've turned out just like my
parents and nagged me for writing so many
useless poems.

Thank you for not sprouting me wings so I could
fly like a dove; at night I'd've had trouble trying
to sleep on my back. Thanks, too, God, for not
turning me into a beautiful movie star; today my
cheeks would be chipmunk puffs of Botox and
thank you, God, too, for not making me President
of the United States of America because the whole
world would despise me for my rabid punditries
against greed, war, poverty, global warming, cruelty
to animals and humans and Daylight Savings Time
and leaving the caps off felt-tip ink markers.

Thanks for not giving me a potato chip factory when
I asked for one at age 12; my lips would've always
been chapped from salt. Thanks, God, for not making
me a honeybee upon the Tundra, an umlaut in Alsace-
Lorraine, a beer can in the garden and thank you most
of all for not making me the lead pitcher for the
Brooklyn Dodgers the summer of 1953 when I thought
I was really a boy because Joe DiMaggio would've
never spoken to me.

Finally, dear God, thank you for never answering any
of my prayers. Making me work so hard being Me kept
me on my toes, my eyes on the road, my back against the
wall, my face in the wind as I awaited the abysses before
the aubauds, repaying my Karmic debt (if, that is, You
believe in Karma, dear God). I needed to toughen up, see,
for what you've got in store for me

Next Time.

148

Picking the Lock on the Door to Paradise
for Fred Voss, 1999

You probably won't believe this but I am
in San Francisco on the corner of Lombard
and Van Ness on the 7th floor of a hotel
overlooking the Golden Gate Bridge and
I am drinking Dom Perignon champagne
and teaching a tall dark and handsome poet
to dance the foxtrot to Frank Sinatra's
"Our Love Is Here to Stay" and this poet
won't do a thing I say, won't let me lead,
won't agree I know what I'm talking about
because I'm a far better dancer because
I was a go-go girl for 7 years, the length
of bad luck time for breaking a mirror.
This poet says he could dance the fox
trot if he wanted to, after all he can twist
and shout to The Doors's "L.A. Woman"
when he wants to but he doesn't want to
dance the foxtrot and when I laugh, he
laughs too and sits down in a chair next to
the window, sips beer and peers out at the
Golden Gate Bridge and I don't give a damn
if he ever learns to dance the foxtrot or the
Blue Danube Waltz, the Charleston, cha-cha,
the Turkey Trot, Funky Chicken or the mambo
or the wa-wa-wa-Watusi or the Lambert Walk
because he's a tall dark handsome poet and
we are in San Francisco peering out at the
Golden Gate Bridge that is disappearing into a
blue-pink sunset fog and our love is here to stay.

. . . And the Ladies of the Fred Astaire Fan Club

When Fred Astaire died, my old go-go girlfriend
Mitzi sent me a sympathy car in which she wrote:
"May Mr. Astaire live in our hearts forever,"
reminding me of our Fred Astaire Fan Club of two
when Mitzi and I were go-go girls in that divy
Daisy Mae's á Go-Go and had to dress like
Daisy Mae in that red polka-dot low-cut top
and dance to that off-key, off-beat psychedelic
band with the LSD-corroded lead singer who
croaked when he did Jimi Hendrix or Morrison.

While my friend and I boogalooed to "Purple Haze"
or "Light My Fire" beneath the black lights that
made our teeth and polka dots glow in the yellow
haze of cigarette smoke, Mitzi and I imagined
we wore marabou, danced the Continental
with Fred Astaire as he crooned "Cheek to Cheek"
so we didn't care when a drunk reached to cop a feel.

Then, at 3 a.m., after we'd emptied and scrubbed
Daisy Mae's thousand ashtrays and beer mugs,
we'd rush home to Fred Astaire and his top hat
on the late-late show on tv, chipper just for us,
just like Betty Grable and her gams for the
WW2 bombardiers, Marianne and her valour
waiting in Marseilles for *les frères*—something fine
for us to come home to after the war.

At the Debbie Reynolds Hollywood Hotel, Las Vegas, Nevada, 1996

In Memoriam: Beautiful. Unsinkable Debbie Reynolds (1932–2016)
and Debbie's daughter Carrie Fisher (1956–2016)

In high school some of the girls I knew carried photos of Debbie
Reynolds in their wallets and wanted to be gym teachers when
they grew up because that's what Debbie'd said in *Photoplay*
she'd wanted to be till she won the Miss Burbank beauty contest
and got rich and famous instead but when those girls in high school
I knew grew up they all got married and had daughters they named
Debbie although Debbie Reynolds' real name was Mary Frances
and those Debbie Daughters had daughters they named Jennifer
and today, here in Las Vegas, Nevada, I sit in the Bogie Bar of the
Debbie Reynolds Hollywood Hotel where giant photos of dead
movie stars hang on the walls: Bogie, Audrey, Joan Crawford,
Johns Garfield and Wayne, Bill Holden, Clark Gable, Cary Grant,
Coop, Marilyn Monroe and more and I watch the girls, maybe
some of the same ones I knew in high school, now much older
grown up women now standing in line to buy tickets to see the
Debbie Reynolds Show, their hair perfectly coifed, grey or dyed
red now or brown or black wearing sequins or leather jackets and
blue jeans or sweats, Nikes or Doc Martens or 5-inch stiletto high
heels while holding hands with their first, second or third husband
some of the girls having had a Liz in their lives too who took away
their First Love, some having gone bankrupt too, forever unsinkable
just like Debbie Reynolds, those girls smoking cigarettes or laughing
or staring straight ahead thinking how soon they'll get to be close
in person to Debbie Reynolds as she sings and dances on stage a
stage like the one they placed her upon in their wallets a 100
decades ago while all the dead movie stars smile down on them
kindly, beautiful gods forgiving those girls for not liking them best.

Heart Attack Poem: A Cognitive Paralysis of Submissive Surreal

Virginia Woolf goes, goes with me down the street as my
husband drives his car fast in half-moonlight midnight
moonglow to the emergency room hospital up the hill,
Virginia Woolf's image on my old sweatshirt, her old
Victorian upswept hairdo soft upon my boom-booming
tora! tora! tora! lightning-attacked heart on December 7,
2016, the 75th anniversary of the Japanese bombing of Pearl
Harbor as my heart finally breaks apart, so it feels, a
ferocious pain inside my chest after all these hectic 76
years I've lived through in this big, bad world and there

in ER proficient nurses and doctors speak a netherworld
alphabet of EKG, IV, OR, ICU, PTSD as they jab, stab and
sting like busy bees in a beehive making not honey but
hurry to make angiogram, nitroglycerin, anesthesia and
morphine while Virginia Woolf does not speak as she's
yanked from my chest, replaced by a clean cotton hospital
gown and placed in a plastic bag for me to wear when I go
home again—if I do—and as they wheel me fast into the
operating room, I wait to hear angels sing, wait to see my
Texas great-grandparents square dance upon the ceiling,
wait for my cowboy grandpa to place me up high one more
time upon his red pony he named Joanie and I wait for
my dead parents to reach for my hand to show me the
way (to where? Heaven? Valhalla? Existential hum?)
as I lay upon the gurney afraid, worried, watching and
wonder Where are they? Why don't they come soothe
me in my paralysis of submissive surreal? What's Next?
I need desperately to ask them so instead I wait to

die

but none of them appear, nor Heaven, nor Valhalla and I do not

die

though I almost do and I live to wear my Virginia Woolf sweat
shirt to ride the wheelchair to my husband's car to take me
home, slowly this time, home, home at last and I'm so glad to see
all that beautiful debris in our small pied a terre near the sea,
see the dusty stacks of books from Beowulf to Virginia Woolf,
our thousands of poems a scattering sweet reality, all of our stuff just
as I left it: my Raggedy Ann doll in a Santa hat, unwrapped Christmas
gifts, unanswered letters and Christmas cards, the disarray so glad
to see me, too, I'm sure: my Andy Warhol Marilyn Monroe tote bag,
the framed Doors first LP on the wall next to Edward Hopper's
"Night Hawks," family photos, all smiling at me, even our bronze
Bukowski head on my roll-top desk smiles—just for me—glad to
see that no bombs broke my Pearl Harbored heart, my ships not
sunk, peace in my paradise as my palm trees and hula skirt
sway aloha, the sea and tides circling my island still blue and
sparkling, even the speechless poinsettias upon my cluttered
coffee table smile bright red, glad to see me, too, and I really,

dear God, I

really like

being alive.

When the music's over

turn out the lights.

—*Jim Morrison*

Poem Notes

"Alley-Walker"
>from *Anthology of American Verse Yearbook of American Poetry,* 1980

"Beer Can in the Garden"
>Accepted by *New York Quarterly* Editor William Packard in 1996 but due to Packard's sudden, lengthy illness and ultimate death, i was not published in NYQ until 2010.

"Endless Summers"
>First Place Winner of *Surfer* magazine 1997 Poetry Competition; Recipient of 2009 Long Beach (CA) City Arts Council Award for permanent display at Long Beach First Street Transit Gallery.

"Getting Drunk with My Third Mother-In-Law"
>from *Best of California Women Poets Anthology,* 1979

"His Poems"
>from *Love Birds,* Chapbook Winner of 1995 Chiron Prize

"The Hollow Cost"
>from *Blood to Remember: American Poets on the Holocaust,* 1991, 2006

"How You Taste the Apples"
>Winner of the Mary Scheirman Poetry Prize, 1995

"Listening to the Radio"
>from *The Habit of Wishing,* 1976 (rewrite, 2016)

"Me and My Mother's Morphine"
>Winner of the 1994 Chiron Poetry Prize

"Picking the Lock on the Door to Paradise"
>from *Picking the Lock on the Door to Paradise,* Winner of the 1999 Nerve Cowboy Chapbook Competition

"The Pow Wow Café"
    from *The Pow Wow Café*, finalist for the 1998 Forward Prize, UK

"Twenty-Ninth Day"
    from *PURR3*, 1974

"Uncle Ray on New Year's Day..."
    Winner of 2012 Philadelphia Poets Prize

CPSIA information can be obtained
at www.ICGtesting.com
Printed in the USA
BVHW03s1439081018
529574BV00009B/1605/P